Optimal Load Management in EV-penetrated Networks: A Metaheuristic Approach with FACTS and DG Support

Smart Solutions for EV-integrated Grids

Published 2026 by River Publishers
River Publishers
Broagervej 10, 9260 Gistrup, Denmark
www.riverpublishers.com

Distributed exclusively by Routledge
605 Third Avenue, New York, NY 10017, USA
4 Park Square, Milton Park, Abingdon, Oxon OX14 4RN

Optimal Load Management in EV-penetrated Networks: A Metaheuristic Approach with FACTS and DG Support: Smart Solutions for EV-integrated Grids / Rupika Gandotra and Kirti Pal.

ISBN 978-87-438-1115-2 (paperback)
ISBN 978-87-438-1118-3 (online)
ISBN 978-8-743-81117-6 (ebook master)
ISBN 978-87-438-1120-6 (ePub)

DOI: 10.1201/9788743811176

Optimal Load Management in EV-penetrated Networks: A Metaheuristic Approach with FACTS and DG Support

Smart Solutions for EV-integrated Grids

Rupika Gandotra
Department of Electrical Engineering,
SoE, Gautam Buddha University, U.P.,
India

Kirti Pal
Department of Electrical Engineering
SoE, Gautam Buddha University, U.P.,
India

River Publishers

Routledge
Taylor & Francis Group
NEW YORK AND LONDON

Contents

Abstract

Optimal Load Management in EV-Penetrated Networks: A Metaheuristic Approach with FACTS and DG Support offers a comprehensive techno-economic assessment and optimization framework for enhancing the performance of power system network through the integration of DG units and flexible AC transmission systems (FACTS) devices, particularly the unified power flow controller (UPFC).

Modern power systems are undergoing rapid transformation due to the widespread integration of renewable distributed generation (DG) sources, the proliferation of electric vehicles (EVs), and the shift toward sustainable and decentralized energy models. While renewable DGs offer significant environmental and economic advantages, their intermittent and stochastic nature poses considerable challenges to grid stability, including voltage fluctuations, frequency deviations, and power flow irregularities. These challenges are further exacerbated by the growing demand from electric transportation, which impose dynamic and unpredictable loads on the network. Therefore, ensuring reliable, stable, and economical power system operation under such complex conditions necessitates advanced optimization and control strategies.

This book presents a explores various distributed sources available and FACTS controllers and how these devices are effectively integrated into the system and managing the loading scenarios due to electric vehicles. A literature work is done on types of distributed sources available and FACTS controller classifications named as series, shunt, shunt-series, and series-series controllers and their impact in power system distribution networks. Furthermore, a review of integration of renewable based sources with FACTS technologies and electric vehicles is provided, highlighting the integration benefits of FACTS controllers with distribution generation into a grid.

The combined use of these technologies aims to improve power flow regulation, voltage profile, load balancing, and overall operational efficiency. To achieve this, two robust meta-heuristic optimization models multi-objective differential evolution (MODE) and an enhanced multi-objective Grey Wolf Optimizer (MOGWO) with opposition-based learning are developed. These models aim to minimize power losses, reduce fuel costs of thermal generators, and lower total economic losses due to electric transportation load, while determining the optimal placement and sizing of DG and UPFC devices. The optimization process is supported by Newton-Raphson power flow analysis and considers multiple objective trade-offs using Pareto optimal front generation under equality and inequality constraints.

The models are evaluated on IEEE-30 bus systems. The results highlight the limitations of the MODE approach as losses were less reduced as compared to enhanced MOGWO, which consistently delivers superior performance. The proposed models have been implemented and tested on a MATLAB 2020a software. This book further explores the optimal fusion of renewable distributed sources with UPFC controller in four different cases. The results show that with the increasing number of DGs and the integration of UPFC devices significantly improves the system's reactive power management, maintaining voltage profiles close to 1.08 per unit, even in the presence of high EV loading cases. This book contributes valuable insights into the design and operation of the smart grids, particularly in optimizing hybrid energy systems with renewable DGs and power electronic interfaces. The developed framework not only reduces operational costs and enhances grid reliability but also supports the environmental sustainability by promoting the efficient use of renewable energy. Moreover, the study emphasizes critical role of meta-heuristic algorithms in addressing complex, multi-constraint optimization problems in modern power systems. The proposed methodology provides a scalable and flexible platform for utility planners and operators, enabling efficient EV load management, improved power quality, and reliable integration of distributed energy resources. The outcomes pave the way for future studies on hybrid optimization techniques real-time energy management, and the incorporation of artificial intelligence and machine learning in power system planning and control.

Preface

The rapid evolution of electric mobility and the increasing penetration of electric vehicles (EVs) into modern power networks present both unprecedented opportunities and pressing challenges. While EVs promise to drive the transition toward cleaner and more sustainable transportation, their widespread adoption imposes significant stress on the existing power infrastructure. The variability of charging demand, the risk of voltage instability, and the increase in network losses demand innovative strategies for optimal load management and system reliability.

This book, *Optimal Load Management in EV-Penetrated Networks: A Metaheuristic Approach with FACTS and DG Support*, is an effort to provide a comprehensive framework to address these challenges. By combining distributed generation (DG) and flexible AC transmission systems (FACTS) devices with advanced multi-objective metaheuristic optimization techniques, such as differential evolution (DE) and Grey Wolf Optimizer (GWO), the book presents novel methodologies for enhancing the performance of EV-integrated power systems. Unlike existing works that often examine EV integration, DG, or FACTS in isolation, this text takes a unified approach to co-optimization reflecting the reality of increasingly complex and interconnected grids.

The book begins by laying the foundations of smart grid architecture, followed by a systematic review of technological advancements in EVs, DG, and FACTS. It then introduces the role of advanced optimization algorithms in solving real-world challenges such as power loss minimization, voltage profile enhancement, and strategic placement of resources. Practical case studies, comparative analyses of algorithms, and discussions on emerging trends ensure that the book not only provides theoretical insights but also serves as a bridge between academic research and practical implementation.

Our aim is to serve multiple audiences: researchers exploring new frontiers in smart grid optimization, practicing engineers seeking practical solutions for EV-induced challenges, policymakers designing sustainable infrastructure, and students aspiring to build expertise in intelligent energy management. We hope this book will contribute meaningfully to advancing sustainable power systems and encourage further innovation in the field.

We express our gratitude to our colleagues, and institutions whose support made this work possible. Most importantly, we thank the academic and professional community, whose collective pursuit of knowledge and innovation continues to inspire us.

Acknowledgement

We wish to extend our sincere gratitude to the individuals whose contributions have played a significant role in the creation of this book. Firstly, we would like to express our deepest appreciation to Professor R. P. Singh, Vice-Chancellor of Gautam Buddha University, for their unwavering support and encouragement throughout this endeavor. Their visionary leadership has provided us with the necessary guidance and motivation to pursue this project.

We are equally grateful to Prof. C. K. Singh, the Registrar, for their administrative support and guidance, which have been essential in facilitating the necessary processes for the completion of this book.

Additionally, we extend our heartfelt thanks to all the esteemed faculty members of the Department of Electrical Engineering. Their expertise, mentorship, and willingness to share knowledge have been invaluable in shaping our understanding and approach to the subject matter of this book.

We also extend our heartfelt thanks to the Staff of River Publishers, Denmark, for their continued support during the press production process of this edited book.

To each individual mentioned above, and to all others who have supported us along the way, we offer our sincerest appreciation. Your contributions have been instrumental, and we are profoundly grateful for the opportunity to collaborate with such esteemed colleagues and mentors.

Abbreviations

ABC	Artificial bee colony
AMI	Advance metering infrastructure
AOA	Archimedes optimization algorithm
ASO	Atom search optimization
BFO	Bacterial foraging optimization
BMO	Barnacles mating optimizer
CSA	Cuckoo search algorithm
DA	Dragonfly algorithm
DE	Differential evolution
DG	Distributed generation
DSC	Distribution static compensator
DSM	Demand side management
EHV	Extra high voltage
EP	Evolutionary programming
EV	Electric vehicle
EVCS	Electric vehicle charging station
FACTS	Flexible ac transmission system
FLFA	Fractional levy flight algorithm
FOA	Firefly optimization algorithm
GA	Genetic algorithm
GSA	Gravitational search algorithm
GUPFC	Generalized unified power flow controller
GWO	Grey wolf optimization
HHO	Harris hawk optimization
IHSA	Improved harmony search algorithm
IPFC	Interline power flow controller
KGMO	Kinetic gas molecule optimization
LCAHA	Levy chaotic artificial hummingbird algorithm

LOSF	Line outage sensitivity factor
MEPSO	Multi-objective evolutionary particle swarm optimization
MFO	Moth-flame optimizer
MGA	Multi-objective genetic algorithm
MMBFO	Multiobjective modified bacterial foraging optimization
MPSO	Multi-objective particle swarm optimization
NSGA-II	Non-dominated sorting genetic algorithm II
ORPD	Optimal reactive power dispatch
PEE	Power electronic equipment
PFA	Pathfinder algorithm
POC	Power oscillation controller
PSO	Particle swarm optimization
PV	Photo voltaic
QCSCA	Quick crisscross sine-cosine algorithm
SSSC	Static synchronous series compensator
STATCOM	Static synchronous compensator
SVC	Static var compensator
TCPAR	Thyristor-controlled phase angle regulator
TCPST	Thyristor-controlled phase shifting transformer
TCSC	Thyristor-controlled series capacitor
TSSR	Thyristor switched series reactor
UPFC	Unified power flow controller

About the Authors

Rupika Gandotra completed her Ph.D. from the Department of Electrical Engineering (EE), Gautam Buddha University, Greater Noida, India, in 2025. Her research focuses on advanced and emerging domains of power and energy systems including renewable energy systems integration, power system analysis and optimization, optimization algorithms and soft computing techniques, smart grid technologies, power electronic controllers, electric vehicles (EV) and EV charging station integration. Her research work addresses real-world challenges in modern power networks, emphasizing sustainability, techno-economic feasibility, and intelligent optimization. She has an impressive publication record in high-impact, peer-reviewed international journals and reputed conferences including SCIE, ESCI, Scopus, IEEE, and IOP indexed platforms.

Kirti Pal is presently working as Associate Professor in Electrical Engineering Department at School of Engineering, Gautam Buddha University, Greater Noida, India. She obtained her B.E. degree from Lakshmi Narain College of Technology, Bhopal, India, M.E. degree from Madhav Institute of Technology & Science, Gwalior, and Ph.D. degree in Electrical Engineering from Rajiv Gandhi Proudyogiki Vishwavidyalaya, Bhopal. She has over 19 years of academic experience and has published many research papers and conference proceedings in various reputed national / international journals. She has guided many B.Tech. and M.Tech. students and two Ph.D. scholars. Pal has also been invited to deliver keynote and expert talks in several national / international conferences and workshops. She was a Guest Editor of *International Journal of Social Ecology and Sustainable Development* for the special issue on Advance Innovation and Technology with Sustainability Engineering (IGI Global,

USA). She has published three books. She serves as a Reviewer for various international journals. She is a Life Member of the Indian Society for Technical Education. Her current interests include restructuring of power system, power system analysis and optimization, renewable energy systems, EVs parameter estimation, and EVs impact analysis on power systems.

CHAPTER

1

Smart Grid Foundations: EVs, DG, and FACTS Integration

1.1 Background

The 21st century has witnessed a transformative shift in energy consumption patterns driven by climate change concerns, advancements in technology, and policy measures aimed at decarbonization. A significant component of this transformation is the electrification of the transportation sector through the adoption of electric vehicles (EVs). EVs are becoming a more environmentally friendly option compared to conventional cars with internal combustion engines (ICE), offering benefits like reduced greenhouse gases, minimum fuel expenses, and enhanced energy efficiency [1-2]. However, the increased adoption of EVs is creating new challenges for electrical power systems. Increased load due to the charging demands of EVs alters the traditional load profile, introduces significant variability in power consumption, and increases peak load requirements. If not addressed properly, this growing demand could overburden the existing generation, transmission, and distribution infrastructure, leading to voltage fluctuations, thermal overload, increased losses, reduced system reliability, and possible outages [3].

To mitigate these challenges, modern power systems must evolve in both structure and function. Two key solutions that offer promise in this context are distributed generation (DG) and flexible AC transmission systems (FACTS) [4-5]. DG refers to small-scale, often renewable, resources (solar photo voltaic (PV), wind, gas turbines) located close to the load centres. DG reduces the stress on the transmission network, improves power quality, and promotes

DOI: 10.1201/9788743811176-1

energy efficiency. Figure 1.1 shows the benefits of DG integration. However, DG units are intermittent and dispersed, requiring intelligent coordination and system support mechanisms [6-7]. Due to the diverse nature of power generation from DG necessitates the integration of advance electrical equipment, such as FACTS controllers, across the system to enhance the performance of a power system network [8-11]. As a result, the integration of electrical components, including DGs, Power Electronic Equipment (PEE), and fuel-based power plants, transforms the distribution grid into a smart grid shown by Figure 1.2. The implementation of advanced power electronic controllers, known as FACTS, marks a significant advancement in power system engineering. These devices are engineered to address the limitations of DG and traditional transmission systems by providing real-time control over power flow and voltage levels.

Figure 1.1 Benefits of DG integration into a power system network.

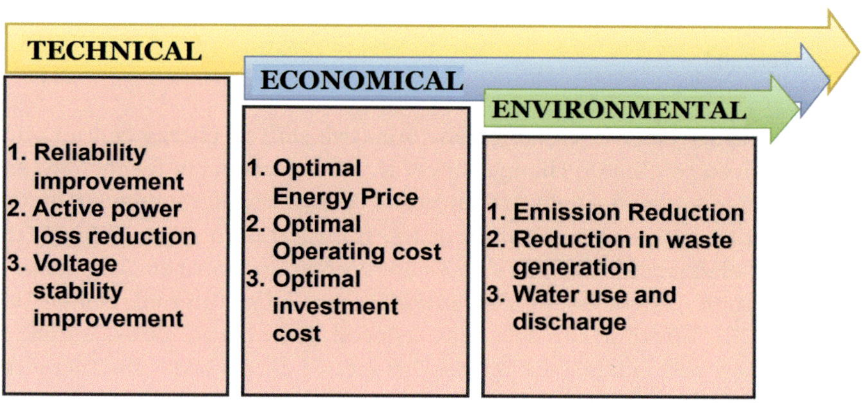

FACTS technology enables the efficient utilization of existing transmission infrastructure, thereby improving system stability and accommodating the increasing demand for electricity. These advanced power-electronic controllers improve the controllability and stability of AC transmission networks. By providing dynamic voltage support, reactive power compensation, and real-time power flow control, FACTS improve grid performance under both normal and stressed operating conditions. Technologies such as Static Synchronous Series Compensator (SSSC), Static Var Compensator (SVC), Static Synchronous Compensator (STATCOM), and Unified Power Flow Controller (UPFC) are widely used to support voltage regulation, increase transmission capacity, and reduce power losses [12-13]. The integration of FACTS devices has been shown to significantly reduce transmission congestion and improve overall system reliability. This has led to increased interest from the power utilities and grid operators in adding FACTS solutions as a part of their grid modernization efforts. As renewable based integration continues to pose challenges for traditional grid infrastructure, FACTS technology is expected to play an increasingly important role in enhancing power quality and system stability. Thus, the integration of DG and FACTS devices in a smart grid environment, particularly in the face of growing EV penetration, offers a holistic solution for managing increased load while enhancing the operational efficiency, flexibility, and economic viability of the power system. This research explores the strategic deployment of these technologies to optimize both the technical and economic aspects of network performance.

Figure 1.2 Conversion of a utility grid into a smart grid.

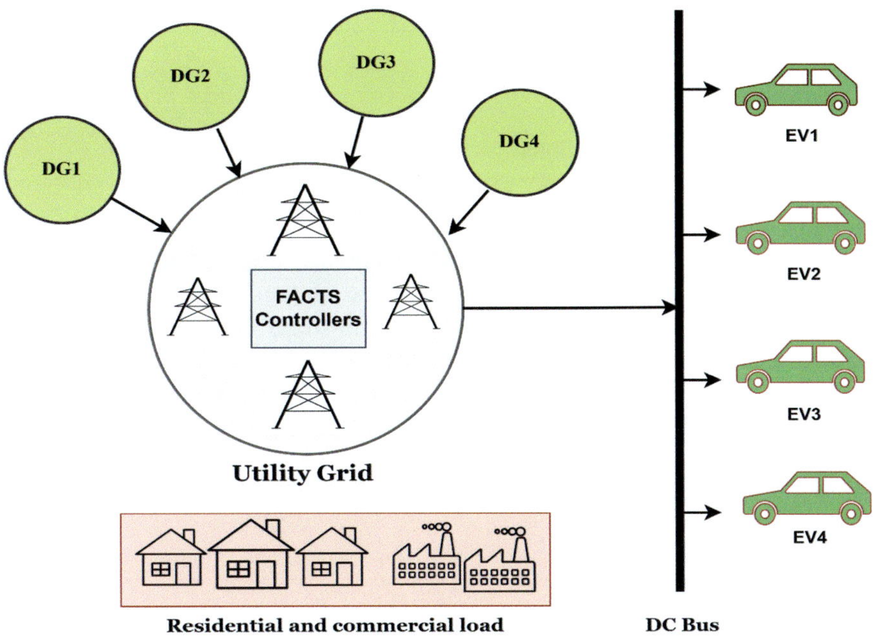

1.2 FACTS Market Growth (2020–2025)

Figure 1.3 describes the global market size for FACTS devices. In the year 2020, the worldwide market for these devices was valued at 1350.5 US$ million, with expectations to grow to 2688.49 US$ million by 2032, indicating a compound annual growth rate of 5.9% over the forecast period.

Figure 1.3 Global FACTS devices market size [14].

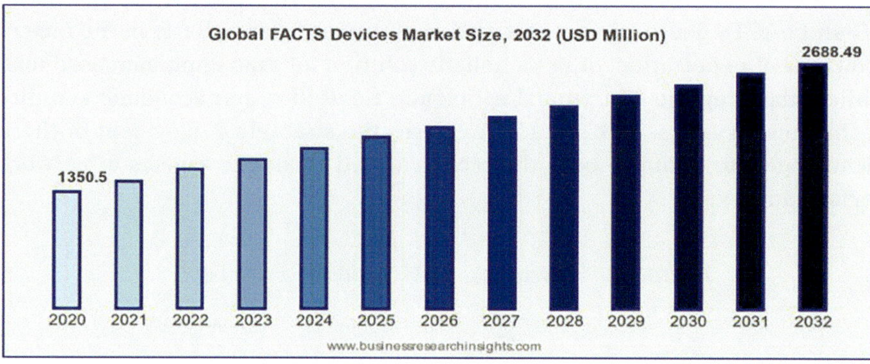

1.3 EVs Growth and Implications

Globally, the EV sector is experiencing rapid growth, fuelled by increased environmental awareness, government incentives, advancements in battery technology, and the decreasing costs of renewable energy sources. According to the International Energy Agency (IEA), the total number of EVs on the road surpassed 17 million globally by 2024, and projections estimate over 50 million EVs by 2030 under the stated policies scenario shown in Figure 1.4. This rapid growth trajectory reflects a paradigm shift in the transportation and energy sectors. This shift is driven by a combination of factors, including stricter emissions regulations, improved charging infrastructure, and evolving customer preferences.

1.3.1 Key Drivers of EV Growth

The growth of EVs is compelled by number of important factors. The main cause is the increasing concern over environmental issues, such as air pollution and climate change, which has led to a global push for cleaner and more sustainable transportation options.

1.3.1.1 Environmental policies and climate targets

Nations worldwide are committing to minimize greenhouse gas emissions to combat climate change. EVs are central to these goals as they eliminate tailpipe emissions and enable integration with clean electricity.

1.3.1.2 Economic incentives

Subsidies, tax credits, and reduced registration or toll charges have made EVs more financially attractive. Additionally, lower operating and maintenance costs contribute to higher consumer adoption.

1.3.1.3 Technological advancements

Improvements in lithium-ion battery technology have increased EV driving range, minimised charging time, and decreased battery costs, making EVs more competitive with ICE vehicles.

1.3.1.4 Urban air quality concerns

Cities suffering from high air pollution levels are adopting EVs as a solution to reduce health risks, especially through the electrification of public transport and commercial fleets.

1.3.1.5 Smart grid and renewable integration

The synergy between EVs and renewable energy sources enhances the sustainability of power systems. EVs can be charged using surplus solar or wind energy, further decarbonizing the grid.

1.3.2 EVs Impact on Power System Load

The growing adoption of EVs presents a transformative shift in energy demand patterns and infrastructure requirements. While EVs contribute positively to decarbonization and sustainability goals, their integration into existing power systems introduces multiple technical and operational challenges [16] as shown by Figure 1.5. Key impacts are detailed as follows.

Figure 1.4 Global EVs sales during period 2015-2024 [15].

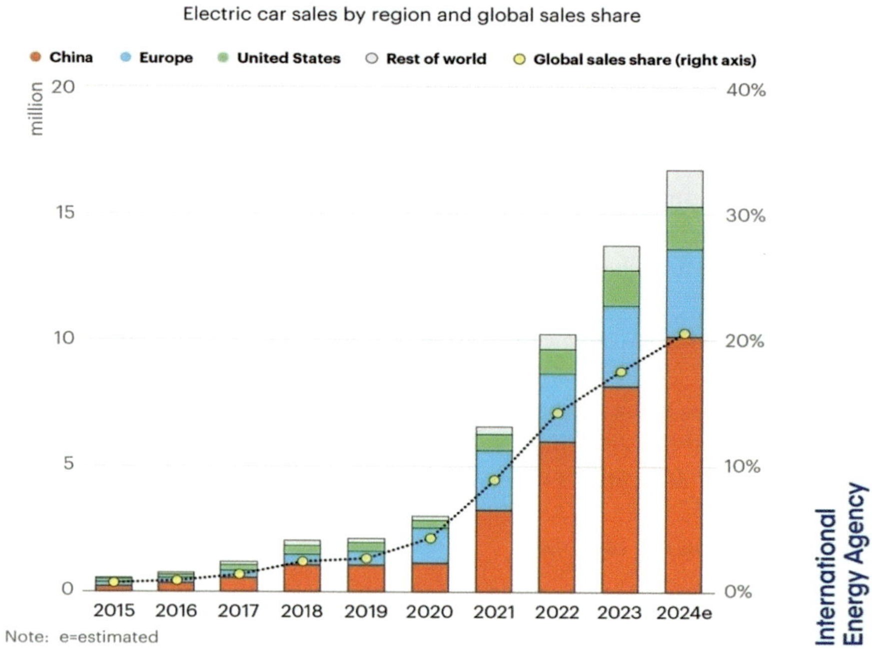

1.3.2.1 Increased peak load demand

The charging of EVs significantly raises the overall demand for electricity. Uncontrolled or simultaneous charging, especially during evening hours when residential demand is also high, can create new peak load periods. This sudden increase in demand may exceed the capacity of local transformers and feeders, leading to system overloads.

1.3.2.2 Load profile distortion

Traditional load curves in power systems follow predictable daily cycles. However, EV charging introduces unpredictable and time-varying demand. As a result, utilities face challenges in accurately forecasting demand, which is crucial for load balancing and generation scheduling.

Figure 1.5 Various factors affected by EV load.

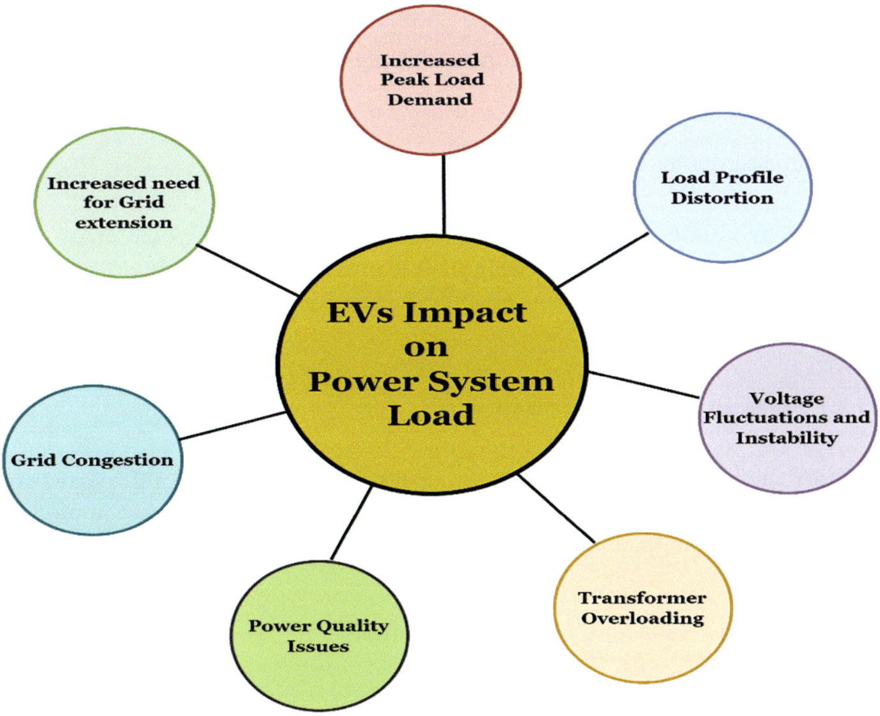

1.3.2.3 Voltage fluctuations and instability

High penetration of EVs, particularly in residential areas at the distribution level, can lead to localized voltage drops and imbalances. Voltage deviation beyond acceptable limits can impair the operation of sensitive equipment and degrade power quality.

1.3.2.4 Transformer overloading

Distribution transformers are often rated based on traditional household loads. When significant number of vehicles are charged at the same time, these transformers may become overloaded, leading to overheating, reduced lifespan, or even failure.

1.3.2.5 Power quality issues

EV chargers, especially fast chargers, act as power electronic loads that can introduce harmonics, voltage flickers, and unbalanced loading into the system. This degrades the power quality and can negatively affect other connected equipment.

1.3.2.6 Grid congestion

Urban distribution networks may experience congestion when many EVs connect to the grid simultaneously. This can result in thermal overloads in cables and substations, limiting the ability of the grid to supply energy reliably and efficiently.

1.3.2.7 Increased need for grid expansion

Utilities may be forced to invest in expensive upgrades to infrastructure, including transformers, cables, substations, and control systems, to accommodate growing EV related loads.

1.4 Possible Solutions for EV Load Management

The rapid growth of EVs presents both opportunities and challenges for modern power systems. EVs introduce significant additional load to the grid, which can be unpredictable and concentrated during peak hours, leading to problems such as transformer overloading, voltage instability, increased power losses, and congestion. Effective load management strategies are required to ensure the reliable and economic operation of power systems shown by Figure 1.6.

1.4.1 Integration of DG

The integration of DG into power systems plays a crucial role in compensating for the additional load introduced by the growing penetration of EVs. As EV adoption increases, the demand on existing power infrastructure rises, potentially leading to voltage instability, increased losses, and overloading of distribution feeders. DG units, such as solar photovoltaic systems, wind turbines, and small-scale gas turbines, can be strategically deployed close to EV charging stations or within the distribution network to supply part of this demand locally. This reduces the burden on central generation and transmission lines, enhances voltage profiles, and improves overall system reliability. Moreover, DG integration facilitates peak load shaving and supports the grid during increased demand periods, making the power system more flexible, resilient, and capable of accommodating the dynamic and decentralized nature of EV charging loads.

1.4.2 Integration of FACTS devices

Adding FACTS devices into the power system is a strategic solution to mitigate the challenges posed by the increasing load from EVs. As EV charging introduces significant variability and stress on the grid, especially during peak hours, FACTS devices such as SSSC, SVC, STATCOM, and UPFC can provide dynamic voltage regulation, reactive power support, and control of power flow. These capabilities help maintain voltage stability, minimise the power losses, and improve the transmission capacity of the grid under high EV load conditions. By enhancing the controllability and flexibility of the power system, FACTS devices enable better integration of EVs without compromising system performance, ensuring reliable and efficient operation even under rapidly changing load scenarios.

1.4.3 Smart charging infrastructure

Smart charging stations are an advanced solution designed to efficiently manage and compensate for the increased load from EVs on the power grid. By enabling features such as load balancing, scheduled charging, and demand response integration, smart charging stations help prevent grid overload during peak hours and promote energy efficiency. To provide clean energy for EVs and reduce the dependency on main grid, they can also work in coordination with energy storage devices and renewable energy sources. Smart charging stations made possible by V2G technology can potentially enables EVs to return electricity to the grid during times of heavy demand, improving system resilience and stability. All things considered, smart charging infrastructure is essential to controlling the effects of EV loads while facilitating a more intelligent and sustainable power system.

1.4.4 Energy Storage Systems (ESS)

To balance demand and supply, lower peak load pressure, and preserve grid stability, ESS stores extra energy during times of low demand or strong renewable output and releases it during peak EV charging periods. Technologies such as lithium-ion batteries, and supercapacitors can be integrated with EV charging infrastructure to provide fast response and reliable energy support. Additionally, ESS enables better utilization of renewable energy sources by mitigating their intermittency and ensuring a consistent power supply for EVs. When combined with smart charging strategies and grid management systems, energy storage enhances the flexibility, reliability, and efficiency of the power network, making it more capable of accommodating large-scale EV deployment without compromising performance.

1.4.5 Demand side management and demand response

Demand side management (DSM) involves modifying consumer electricity usage patterns through energy-efficient practices and load control measures, while demand response (DR) enables consumers to reduce or shift their electricity usage in response to grid signals, pricing incentives, or peak demand periods. By encouraging EV owners to charge during off-peak hours or when renewable generation is high, DSM and DR help flatten load curves, minimise peak demand, and eliminate stress on the power system. Advanced metering infrastructure and smart grid technologies play a key role in implementing these strategies by enabling real-time communication between utilities and EV users. Overall, DSM and DR enhance grid flexibility and stability, making the integration of EVs more sustainable and cost-effective.

Figure 1.6 Various strategies for EV load management.

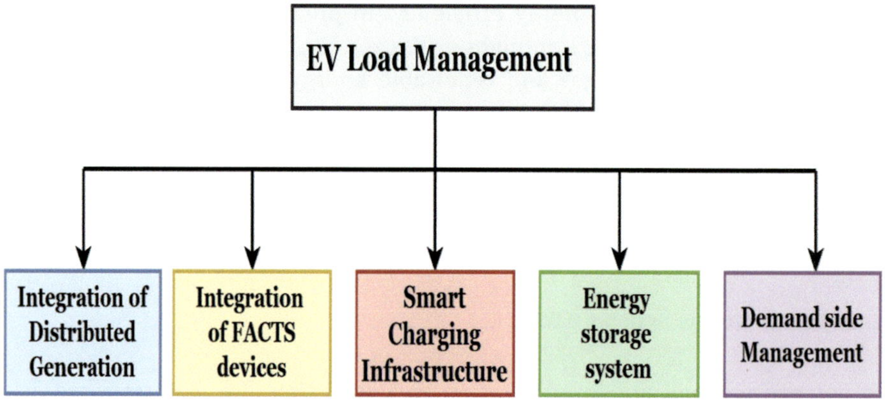

1.5 Combined Role of DG and FACTS in Smart EV-Integrated Grids

The smart grid represents an evolution of the traditional power system through the integration of advanced communication, automation, and control technologies to enhance reliability, efficiency, and sustainability. In the context of increasing EV adoption, the smart grid must be capable of accommodating high and often unpredictable loads without compromising stability or power quality. This necessitates the deployment of both DG and FACTS in a complementary and coordinated manner.

1.5.1 Local load support and grid relief

One of the primary challenges introduced by EVs is the concentration of load at the distribution level, especially during peak charging periods. DG units, such as rooftop solar PV, small wind turbines, and microturbines, can be strategically deployed near EV charging stations to supply part of the load locally. This reduces the burden on upstream transmission and distribution infrastructure. FACTS devices, such as STATCOMs or SVCs, complement this by dynamically regulating voltage and reactive power, ensuring the power from DG is effectively integrated without destabilizing the local grid.

1.5.2 Voltage stability enhancement

Voltage instability is a key concern in areas with high EV penetration. EV charging can cause sudden voltage drops or fluctuations, particularly on weaker or unbalanced feeders. FACTS devices provide rapid reactive power compensation, stabilizing voltage profiles in real time. Simultaneously, DG can help by supplying real power, reducing the need to draw energy from distant sources. The synergy between local active power support from DG and reactive power management from FACTS ensures a balanced and stable voltage environment.

1.5.3 Improved power flow and load management

DG changes the traditional unidirectional power flow model of the grid into a more complex, bidirectional flow scenario. While this increases flexibility, it also adds complexity to power system operation. FACTS devices such as UPFC can be used to manage power flow actively by controlling line impedance, voltage magnitude, and phase angle. This allows for optimal routing of power from both centralized plants and distributed resources, including EV chargers and DG units, preventing line overloads and bottlenecks.

1.5.4 Enhanced system resilience and reliability

The presence of DG in a distributed architecture adds resilience by reducing dependency on central power plants and enabling localized energy autonomy during outages. In the event of faults or grid disturbances, DG units can operate in islanded mode (microgrids), maintaining critical loads like EV chargers. FACTS devices, through fast control capabilities, can dampen system oscillations, improve fault ride-through performance, and prevent cascading failures, thereby enhancing the robustness of the entire grid.

1.5.5 Support for renewable energy and clean EV charging

As many DG systems are based on renewable energy sources (PV and wind), their integration aligns with clean EV charging goals. However, the variability and intermittency of renewables can create power quality issues. FACTS devices can mitigate these fluctuations by rapidly compensating for imbalances and harmonics. For instance, STATCOM can help smooth out the voltage variations caused by intermittent solar input while EVs are being charged. Together, DG and FACTS enable a low-carbon and high-quality energy supply for transportation.

1.5.6 Optimized asset utilization and deferred infrastructure investment

Combined use of DG and FACTS allows utilities to optimize the performance of existing assets. DG reduces the loading on central generators and long-distance transmission lines, while FACTS ensures efficient utilization of the existing grid by controlling power flow and voltage profiles. This integrated approach delays or even eliminates the need for costly upgrades to substations, transformers, and conductors, offering a cost-effective solution to accommodate EV growth.

1.5.7 Real-time control and smart grid integration

In a smart grid environment, real-time data from EVs, DG units, and FACTS devices can be collected and analysed using Advance Metering infrastructure (AMI) and Internet of Things (IoT) platforms. Such coordination ensures optimal system performance, reduced operational costs, and increased system visibility and control.

1.6 Need for Economic Assessment and Optimization

As the power sector undergoes a profound transformation driven by the growth of EVs, renewable energy sources, and advanced technologies like FACTS, the challenges faced by power system planners and operators are no longer solely technical in nature. One of the most critical aspects of modern power system planning is the economic dimension ensuring that the solutions adopted not only improve system performance but also do so in a cost-effective, sustainable, and optimized manner.

1.6.1 Rising costs due to load growth and EV integration

The widespread adoption of EVs contributes significantly to load growth, particularly in urban and residential areas. This increased demand leads to Overloading of distribution feeders and substations, higher power losses and operational inefficiencies. Traditionally, utilities would address this by expanding capacity installing new transformers, reinforcing feeders, or adding reactive power support. However, these methods are capital-intensive and may not offer optimal cost-benefit ratios, especially when compared to smarter alternatives like DG and FACTS devices.

1.6.2 Cost-effectiveness of FACTS and DG solutions

FACTS devices such as SSSC, SVC, STATCOM, and Thyristor Controlled Series Capacitor (TCSC) offer fast and flexible solutions for voltage control, power flow regulation and system stability enhancement. Similarly, DG can provide localized energy support, reduce transmission losses, and defer grid upgrades. However, these technologies come with significant capital, operation, and maintenance costs. Thus, simply installing FACTS and DG is not sufficient; their type, location, size, and timing must be economically optimized to maximize returns on investment while ensuring grid reliability.

1.6.3 Need for integrated economic optimization

The deployment of FACTS and DG involves balancing multiple objectives such as loss minimization, voltage regulation, reliability, and cost. Economic optimization helps navigate these trade-offs effectively. FACTS and DG devices have system-wide impacts in that a poorly placed STATCOM can affect voltage profiles in neighbouring buses or cause control instability. Economic optimization ensures coordinated deployment. With emerging EV adoption and renewable penetration, future load profiles and generation availability are uncertain. Optimization models can incorporate scenarios and probabilistic methods to design robust and cost-effective solutions.

1.6.4 Relevance to modern smart grids

Smart grids of the future require solutions that are not just technically effective but economically rational. Grid modernization involves significant investment in digital infrastructure, automation, and advanced devices. Economic optimization is critical for making the grid more resilient to demand shocks (e.g., sudden EV load increase) and attracting private investment in renewable and grid-support technologies.

1.7 Motivation of this Study

The global transition toward cleaner transportation systems has accelerated the adoption of EVs across residential, commercial, and public sectors. This shift, while environmentally beneficial, has introduced significant challenges for Particle Swarm Optimization (PSO), particularly in terms of load management, voltage stability, power quality, and infrastructure adequacy. As the number of EVs connected to the grid increases, so does the stress on existing power distribution and transmission networks many of which were not originally designed to handle such dynamic and localized demand surges.

1.7.1 Rapid growth of EVs

The increasing adoption of EVs globally is leading to significant new electrical load on power systems, especially during peak charging hours.

1.7.2 Stress on existing power infrastructure

Traditional transmission and distribution networks were not originally designed to handle sudden and concentrated EV charging loads, resulting in issues like voltage instability, increased losses, and potential overloading.

1.7.3 Need for cost-effective solutions

Conventional methods like grid reinforcement and transformer upgrades are capital-intensive and time-consuming, necessitating more flexible and economical alternatives.

1.7.4 Emergence of FACTS devices and DG

FACTS devices improve voltage regulation, stability, and power transfer capabilities, while DG helps reduce transmission losses and supports local demand.

1.7.5 Lack of integrated planning approaches

Most existing studies either focus on FACTS or DG independently and often neglect the economic optimization of their combined use, particularly in EV-rich environments.

1.7.6 Economic constraints in grid expansion

Utilities and regulators often face limited financial resources, making it essential to maximize the return on investments through optimized planning.

1.7.7 Multi-objective optimization requirement

Balancing technical performance (e.g., loss reduction, voltage profile improvement) with economic feasibility demands a well-structured, multi-objective optimization approach.

1.7.8 Gap in existing literature

There is a lack of comprehensive studies that incorporate EV-induced load modelling, economic assessment, and coordinated deployment of FACTS and DG.

1.7.9 Support for smarter grid evolution

The study contributes to the vision of a smart, flexible, and future-ready grid capable of integrating EVs, renewables, and advanced control technologies effectively.

1.7.9.1 Environmental and policy alignment

Optimizing power system performance using efficient technologies supports sustainability goals and aligns with global policies aimed at decarbonizing energy and transportation sectors.

CHAPTER

2

Technological Landscape: EVs, DG, and FACTS in Smart Grids

2.1 Introduction

This chapter provides background information and an introduction to the optimal location and sizing of DGs, FACTS controllers and Electric Vehicle Charging Stations (EVCS) within the distribution network. It covers various aspects of distribution network, including reduction of power losses, fuel prices of thermal generators and voltage deviation. The discussion encompasses both DG and FACTS controllers, highlighting the associated challenges. The chapter further delves into the impact of EVCS loading on the distribution network, along with DG-FACTS. The section concludes with an examination of the challenges specifically related to renewable energy-based distribution grid, followed by a review of prior research in the field. Optimal location and sizing in distribution networks are pivotal for achieving an efficient, reliable, and sustainable energy distribution system. Through the strategic placement and sizing of electrical equipment, utilities can enhance operational efficiency, reduce energy losses, and ensure a high-quality power delivery to consumers. As the energy landscape evolves, it becomes increasingly essential to employ advanced tools and methodologies to tackle the complexities of distribution network optimization and make informed decisions that benefit both utilities and end-users.

The energy landscape has seen unique advancements because of the quick adoption of renewable energy sources. Traditionally, electricity is produced using non-conventional sources of energy, such as coal, oil, and gas. The energy

DOI: 10.1201/9788743811176-2

produced creates significant CO_2 emissions with high generation costs. Hence, to reduce the usability of fossil fuel energy sources and eliminate the unfavourable effects of climate change, scientists are developing and maximizing renewable energy solutions [17]. Besides residential and industrial load, the recent trend of increasing number of EVs on the road has also put a burden on the electricity industry. Thus, distribution grids have evolved into smart grids by the addition of power electrical equipment such as DG units, power electronic components, and EVCS. It is difficult for a PSO to provide sustainable power quality under such stressful conditions. However, the employment of renewable-based DG can solve the problem of load demand by providing clean energy with low-cost production. However, owing to the varying nature of generation, it is important to integrate power electronic equipment such as FACTS controllers across the system so that the system's performance is enhanced [18].

Advanced power electronic controllers FACTS have marked a pivotal advancement in power system engineering, and these devices are designed to address the limitations of conventional transmission systems by enabling real-time control over power flow and voltage profiles. FACTS technology facilitates the optimal utilization of the existing transmission infrastructure, thereby enhancing system stability and accommodating the growing demand for electricity [19]. The STATCOM controller is based on voltage-source converter technology, which offers the fastest response time and superior performance in voltage regulation under different system conditions [20-22]. SSSC is a series compensator that is utilized to control impedance of the branch lines, thereby optimizing the power flow and enhancing the transfer capability of the network. These devices are particularly effective in managing line congestion and improving system stability. UPFC comes in the category of combined devices (series-parallel controllers) and Interline Power Flow Controller (IPFC) is series-series combined controllers.

UPFC integrate functionalities of both series and shunt compensation. UPFC controllers can independently regulate the magnitude of voltage, vary impedance and phase angle, provide comprehensive control over the flow of power, and significantly enhance network's flexibility [23]. Other power-related issues, such as voltage drop, voltage swell, flickering, and harmonic distortions, also significantly impact the power system's performance and reliability. FACTS is an advanced technology that is used to control and stabilize power networks. These devices effectively manage the power quality by dynamically regulating the voltage levels, compensating for the reactive power, and mitigating harmonic issues. FACTS devices improve power quality by ensuring a consistent voltage profile, reducing distortions, and enhancing the overall system efficiency by adjusting the transmission line parameters [24].

On the other hand, the rising demand of power such as adoption of EVs can lead to concentrated charging demands in specific areas and at certain times, potentially overwhelming the local distribution infrastructure. Without proper planning and management, this could result in voltage fluctuations, transformer overloads, and increased system losses. Therefore, it is crucial to plan the distribution grid with optimal sizing of electrical equipment and load management techniques to provide stable power and avoid detrimental impacts on the grid.

2.2 Metaheuristic Techniques

Metaheuristic optimization, grounded in mathematical principles, has been applied to address numerous complicated and multi-objective challenges. They provide an adequate solution to any complex problem, whereas traditional optimization may find it difficult to obtain an optimum solution for a problem that is nonlinear and complex. These techniques integrate fundamental heuristic concepts, such that the exploration and exploitation of a research area is effective. For example, the Harris Hawk Optimization (HHO) [25] technique provides proper size, number, and accommodation of DG units in case 33 and 69 power networks to minimize power losses. This HHO technique was also tested on benchmark functions. A hybrid approach of the Genetic Algorithm (GA) and JAYA algorithm (JA) is utilized to integrate DG units (solar and wind) to reduce power losses and voltage fluctuations. The findings indicate that the hybrid approach provides better results than other approaches, such as PSO, SLFA, and JA [26]. The hybrid methodology integrates AGPSO-GWO techniques for the optimum location of FACTS controllers such as UPFC, SVC, and TCSC to accelerate gains in the system efficiency and operation [27]. Pareto solutions were used to compare the multi-objective techniques PSO and Cuckoo Search Algorithm (CSA) for power loss minimization with UPFC installation [28]. The combination of PSO with Kinetic Gas Molecule Optimization (KGMO) for the optimal distribution of FACTS controllers improves stability [29]. WOA was applied to cases 14 and 30 bus systems to reduce the operating cost of the system using the optimal accommodation and dimensions of the FACTS controllers. WOA is further compared with GA and PSO [30]. Several methods are available for improving the efficiency of optimization algorithms. In [31], PSO performance and strength were accelerated with the involvement of Shannon entropy with fractional calculus methods to handle optimal load flow problems such as system power loss minimization, improvement in voltage, and overall cost minimization.

With the addition of FACTS devices such as UPFC, SVC, TCSC, and STATCOM optimized by the Artificial Bee Colony (ABC) algorithm [32] on case

14 and 30 bus systems improved the system's loadability by reducing the power losses. FACTS controllers-based optimal load flow is performed to enhance the power network's stability using the YYPO technique [33], which also proves that, with the employment of STATCOM, UPFC and IPFC controllers, system security significantly increases. The power transfer capability of bus systems 30 and 57 is increased with the use of the modified lightning attachment procedure optimization (MLAPO) approach after the best positioning of FACTS devices, resulting in an effective improvement of network performance [34].

Another technique, Atom Search Optimization (ASO), improves system security while performing the best placement of FACTS controllers [35]. ASO is compared with other techniques, such as Dragonfly Algorithm (DA), WOA, and Grey Wolf Optimization (GWO). The static Var compensator is optimally placed using a MOBFO to minimize losses and voltage deviation. A MOGA technique is used for reactive power planning by placing the FACTS controller and capacitor banks with Pareto solutions [36]. Fuel cost minimization and power loss reduction was effectively performed on the IEEE-30 bus system with the development of the PSO technique [37]. Various control parameters are modified using the PSO technique to obtain the intended objective functions. The power controlling capability of FACTS controllers is utilized when optimal placement is performed using a modified KGMO approach with Pareto solutions. The results were compared to those of the PSO approach to verify the superiority of the KGMO technique [38]. The ability of the GWO technique is accelerated when PSO is integrated. This combination of GWO and PSO is optimizing the various control variables such that active losses minimization and voltage deviation reduction are obtained [39]. Differential Evolution (DE) was used on bus system case 30 to enhance the voltage across buses and reduce system losses when FACTS controllers were optimally placed. The results were compared with FACTS and without FACTS for increased loading conditions [40]. Fractional Levy Flight Algorithm (FLFA) was applied to reduce power losses and improvement of voltage index when DGs were incorporated with FACTS controllers [41]. The fuel cost of conventional generators was reduced when the power flow from generators was optimized using the SHADE algorithm. In addition, the ideal placement and sizing of FACTS controllers were determined [42].

2.3 Renewable-Based DG

Renewable-based DG has emerged as a transformative component of modern power systems, aiming to decentralize energy production while promoting sustainability and reducing dependency on fossil fuels. DG is defined as small-to-medium scale power sources placed near the area of consumption, thereby mitigating transmission losses, enhancing overall grid ability, and reliability [43]. DGs can be distinguished into different types. First, those which supply only real power are considered type-1. Second, those designed to provide only reactive power to enhance the voltage profile are considered type-2. Third, those that have the capability to deliver both real and reactive power are considered type-3. Finally, those that supply real power while absorbing reactive power are considered type-4. Among various renewable DG technologies, solar photovoltaic (PV), wind turbines, and biomass plants are the most prominent.

These sources offer low operational costs and environmental benefits but introduce operational challenges due to their intermittent and uncertain nature [44]. Solar and wind power, in particular, exhibit variability influenced by weather conditions, necessitating sophisticated grid integration strategies and robust voltage regulation mechanisms [45-46]. Effective integration of renewable DG requires addressing reactive power support, voltage stability, and system losses. Optimal Reactive Power Dispatch (ORPD) is a key tool in this context, optimizing control variables like generator voltages, transformer tap positions, and reactive power injection devices to enhance power quality and maintain voltage stability [47-48]. However, the ORPD problem is inherently non-linear and non-convex, complicated further by the stochastic nature of renewable generation [49].

To manage these complexities, several meta-heuristic algorithms were employed. Techniques such as GA, Firefly Optimization Algorithm (FOA), Archimedes Optimization Algorithm (AOA), and Pathfinder Algorithm (PFA) have shown promise in efficiently solving the ORPD problem in systems that are integrated with renewable DGs [50]. Each algorithm presents distinct advantages: for instance, GA demonstrates strong global search capabilities, while AOA offers high solution precision. Moreover, the unpredictability of renewable generation is often modelled using probability density functions Weibull distribution for wind speed and lognormal distribution for solar irradiance to accurately represent their variability and assess their impact on power system performance [51-52]. Simulation studies using IEEE standard bus systems have validated these approaches, showing significant reductions in power loss, voltage deviation, and improved voltage stability indices when renewable DGs are optimally placed [53-54]. Despite installation costs and integration complexities, renewable DG presents a long-term solution for sustainable and resilient energy systems. Advances in converter technology, including smart inverters capable of real-time voltage and frequency control, further enhance the viability of renewable-based DG in modern grids [55]. As the penetration of renewable DG increases, continued research into uncertainty modelling, optimization strategies, and grid compatibility remain vital.

2.3.1 Optimal location and sizing of DG

The placement of DG into distribution systems plays a pivotal role in minimizing power losses, enhancing voltage profiles, enhancing reliability, and deferring infrastructure upgrades. However, the accommodation and sizing of DGs must be optimized to avoid adverse effects such as voltage rise, reverse power flow, and protection miscoordination. Numerous studies have addressed this optimization problem using various analytical and meta-heuristic techniques.

Early optimization approaches used teaching-learning-based optimization (TLBO), which offered parameter independence and fast convergence. Despite these benefits, TLBO sometimes converges to local optima, especially in complex systems with multiple constraints [56]. Reference [57] emphasized multi-DG placement in primary distribution networks for minimizing real power loss. Their study highlighted that coordinated sizing and siting of DGs considering both active and reactive power injection significantly enhances system performance. Similarly, [58] introduced ALOA for optimal allocation of renewable-based DGs and showed its effectiveness on radial distribution systems.

A comprehensive framework for optimal placement considering system topology, load distribution, and multiple types of DGs is proposed in [59]. Their multi-objective approach aimed at minimizing loss, maximizing reliability, and managing investment cost. Reference [60] further examined the impact of various DG types in microgrids, revealing their influence on performance indices under different scenarios. Several studies have also incorporated economic considerations into the optimization framework. Reference [61] combined technical metrics like voltage profile and power loss with economic parameters such as installation cost. Godha et al. [62] conducted a review of heuristic algorithms for DG placement, offering valuable insights into selection criteria based on network conditions.

Recent hybrid approaches have yielded improved convergence and solution quality. Moradi and Abedini [63] introduced a GA–PSO hybrid that outperformed single-algorithm techniques in identifying optimal locations and sizes. Bagheri et al. [64] demonstrated that combining different DG types each with unique power characteristics can yield better loss reduction outcomes than using a single type. Furthermore, for networks with complex load dynamics, analytical methods such as the one proposed by [65] can provide near-optimal solutions, although they may be computationally intensive. Their application of the FA demonstrated the outstanding performance in optimizing both size and placement of multiple DG types across IEEE-33, 69 bus systems. FA was shown to outperform PSO in achieving lower power loss with smaller DG sizes and improved voltage profiles. Analytical validation further confirmed FA's efficiency, reinforcing its suitability for medium-scale systems.

2.4 Flexible Alternating Current Transmission Systems

Advances in power electronic technology have enabled devices like FACTS [66]. FACTS are particularly useful tools for linked systems to improve various stability issues, increase transfer capacity, and manage power flow. To better understand FACTS devices and their optimal operation and planning within power systems, several scholars have looked at various models and techniques [67-69]. The FACTS family can improve power transfer capacity, stability, and controllability. Power system components such as transistors, thyristors, transformers, reactors, switches, and capacitors are combined in these devices. Applications requiring high power can be handled by thyristors with high current ratings. The dynamic and transient performance of the power system is also improved by the FACTS controller.

FACTS devices have electronic-based switches that enhance transmission capacity, controllability, voltage stability, and transient stability. Their usage can result in a 40-50% increase in transmission capacity, and they are sensitive and versatile [70]. The FACTS controller enables electricity transmission across a transmission line near its thermal rating. The standard coupling and AC bus points in FACTS devices are where the apparent admittance and impedance are altered. Local reactive or capacitive current is supplied, AC components are added to power system network nodes, and the corresponding driving point impedance at the interface is altered via controlled switching.

2.4.1 Classifications of FACTS

2.4.1.1 Series controllers

The serial controller can be any variable impedance with fundamental, sub-synchronous, and harmonic frequencies, such as a static converter, reactor, condenser. All serial controllers inject a voltage in series with the transmission line since a fluctuating impedance in series multiplied by the current flow signals a serial voltage injected into the line as shown in Figure 2.1.

The serial controller injects or uses reactive power only when the voltage and line current are in quadrature. For any other phase combination, active power management will also be employed. Thus, controlling the current in the transmission line is the main purpose of this type of equipment. The first controller to be established in India was TCSC. Voltage stability is provided by FACTS controllers by varying impedance and enhancing power quality. The features and cost comparison of several FACT controllers have been covered by [71]. There are four types of FACT controllers: series, shunt, series-series, and series-shunt. Power transmission capabilities of lines are enhanced by series controllers. A series controller may take the shape of a reactor, changeable capacitor, or varied power. A series compensator based on a voltage source is called an SSSC [72]. This regulates the transmittable power and line voltage drop and enhances the lines' maximum power transmission as a result. When a defect occurs in a distance relay, the SSSC performances are examined by [73] at different points, such as far end, middle of the line, and end of the line. The Thyristor Switched Series Reactor (TSSR), an inductive reactance compensator that offers stepwise control, was covered by [74].

Figure 2.1 Block diagram of series FACTS controllers.

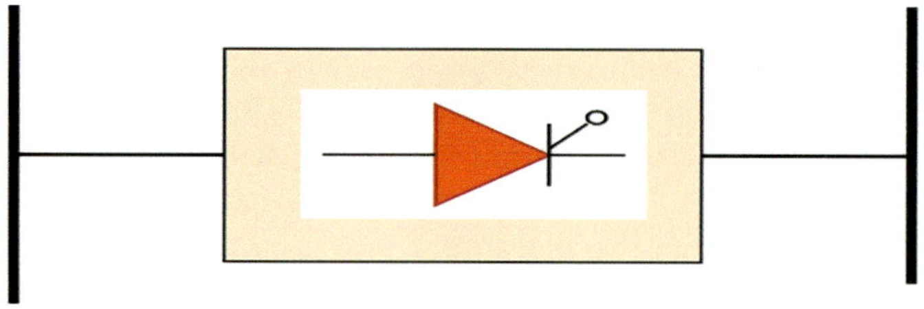

2.4.1.2 Parallel controllers

A parallel controller is responsible for controlling voltage at a particular node with the injection of reactive current whereas, in the case of serial controllers, they require separate controllers to be installed in each line, in case line failure happens. Hence, the basic idea behind a parallel controller is to supply the line with reactive power to boost real power flow by increasing its power factor while keeping voltage levels within safe bounds even in the face of severe loads as shown in Figure 2.2. For example, STATCOM is the parallel controller which is responsible for managing reactive power flow across the lines. A detailed analysis of STATCOM, which is placed in a five-bus power system, may be found in [75].

When STATCOM is installed in the transmission line, the shunt controller injects power to provide the desired power flow rates of 0.43 pu and 0.154 pu, respectively. Additionally, correction strategies provide a decrease in transmission line loading. Additionally, to enhance voltage management, a parallel compensator is introduced at bus 4. In these cases, all bus voltages fall inside the voltage limits. A detailed discussion of the use of two control techniques to improve transmission stability with Shunt linked FACTS controllers can be found in [76]. For a conventional cascade controller, which consists of an inner vector-current controller and many outer-control loops, a STATCOM parallel controller is used. Reference [77] describes a power system network that is simulated in three stages using the MATLAB environment: STATCOM only, without, and STATCOM with Power Oscillation Controller (POC). The outcome demonstrates that, in the event of a malfunction, the system parameters will become unstable in the absence of STATCOM. The author of [78] suggests that STATCOM could produce power and function as a capacitance if the system was running at low voltage. STATCOM will absorb reactive power and function as an inductive device when the system voltage is operating at a high level. The SVC controller was employed to investigate ways to enhance the transient stability of the selected model. Thyristor switches, which function as a sort of phase shifting transformer, control Thyristor-Controlled Phase Shifting Transformer (TCPST) or Thyristor Controlled Phase Angle Regulator (TCPAR) to offer an instantaneous change in phase angle. Reactive power in branch lines is compensated with shunt controllers.

Figure 2.2 Block diagram of shunt FACTS controllers.

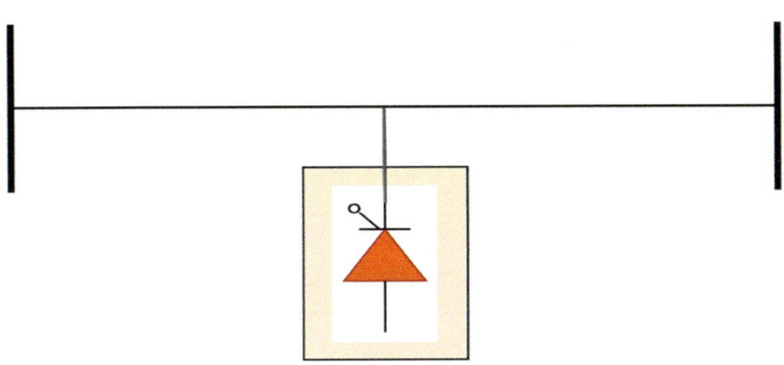

2.4.1.3 Combined series-shunt controllers

In the series-shunt controller combination, both series and shunt controller types are utilized. Using a series-shunt controller to supply current to the lines and a shunt controller to regulate voltage is the fundamental idea behind this type of controller. When the controllers are installed simultaneously in a system, active power is transferred between them. Series-shunt controllers are used to regulate both active and reactive power, which enhances system performance. UPFC is an example of a series-shunt controller. The specific constructional elements of UPFC, which is a combination of SSSC and STATCOM, are covered in [79]. According to the discussion in [80], UPFC may be utilized to enhance power condition by managing both actual and reactive power.

By regulating transmission line reactance, magnitude of voltage, and phase angle with wind energy generation, UPFC application may regulate power flow in branch lines [81]. These two controllers are placed in series with a line via a DC connection to improve two-way power flow for active and reactive power adjustment. Three converters, two in series and one in parallel with the line, make up the smart power system characteristics that Generalized Unified Power Flow Controller (GUPFC) regulates for the line, including power flows, bus voltage, actual power, and reactive power. When parallel and series compensators are combined, they may be utilized to modify system characteristics, including increasing the power transmission capacity, as suggested by [82].

2.4.1.4 Combined series-series controllers

This combination arises from the addition of two or more series controllers together in the lines. Reactive power compensation across lines is the primary function of series controllers, however these controllers may also deliver actual power between lines via power connections. The controller can balance the flow of both reactive and actual power because of its power transfer capabilities. A combined series-series controller is called IPFC. One of the voltage source converters, it regulates the power flow in systems with several transmission lines. Usually, they are positioned on transmission lines that are extremely dangerous.

2.4.2 Optimal location and sizing of FACTS devices in power systems

In recent decades, FACTS have become central to resolving complex challenges in power systems, especially with increasing renewable energy integration and fluctuating load demands. FACTS devices enhance voltage regulation, reduce transmission losses, stabilize frequency, and improve the overall security and efficiency of the grid. However, due to their high capital and operational costs, determining the optimal location and sizing of these devices is essential to ensure cost-effectiveness while achieving maximum system benefits [83].

The primary objective of FACTS placement is to achieve technical and economic improvements, including reduced active power losses, enhanced voltage profiles, and better system stability margins. Traditional methods, such as analytical or sensitivity-based techniques, initially addressed this by assessing system performance indices. These methods rely on Jacobian matrices and sensitivity factors to determine the impact of FACTS on key metrics like voltage deviation and loss indices. However, their applicability is often limited to small or moderately sized networks due to computational limitations.

To overcome the shortcomings of deterministic methods, optimization-based approaches were introduced. Conventional optimization techniques such as linear programming (LP), nonlinear programming (NLP), and Newton-Raphson-based methods provided structured frameworks but were often hindered by convergence issues and local minima problems in complex power systems [84]. As the system size and complexity grew, the research community shifted toward metaheuristic and hybrid optimization techniques due to their flexibility, adaptability, and superior performance in exploring large and nonlinear search spaces. Metaheuristic algorithms such as GA, PSO, DE, SA, and Harmony Search have been widely adopted to solve the FACTS allocation problem. GA, inspired by natural evolution, is known for its capability to explore wide search spaces and has been effectively used for multi-objective optimization of FACTS parameters in IEEE bus systems [85-86]. PSO, derived from the collective behaviour of bird flocks, has shown faster convergence and better handling of continuous variables, proving effective in minimizing power losses and improving voltage stability when placing devices like SVC and TCSC [87].

DE, introduced by Storn and Price, enhances global exploration by leveraging population-based difference vectors and has been utilized successfully for sizing and locating UPFC to optimize multiple objectives simultaneously [88]. Simulated annealing mimics the annealing process in metallurgy and excels at escaping local optima. It has been particularly useful in combinatorial FACTS placement scenarios involving discrete settings and locations [89]. Similarly, the Tabu Search algorithm, with its adaptive memory mechanism, enables efficient search of feasible spaces and avoids cycling through visited solutions, making it robust for large-scale grid systems [90].

Beyond individual techniques, hybrid approaches that combine the precision of analytical methods with the exploration capabilities of metaheuristics have emerged as powerful tools. These approaches use sensitivity analysis to reduce the solution space before applying evolutionary algorithms to fine-tune device parameters, significantly improving computational efficiency [91]. Recent works also incorporate fuzzy logic and artificial intelligence frameworks, enabling the handling of vague constraints and system uncertainties particularly relevant for grids with high penetration of intermittent renewables [92]. Moreover, recent developments have focused on multi-objective optimization techniques, where goals like minimizing cost, reducing losses, enhancing voltage stability, and maximizing loadability are considered simultaneously. For example, hybrid GA-PSO algorithms have been used to optimize the placement of UPFC and STATCOM devices while balancing installation costs and technical performance [93].

The use of Evolutionary Programming (EP), BFOA, and GWO have also expanded due to their effectiveness in complex multi-modal problems encountered in modern smart grids [94-95]. Several studies demonstrate the application of these techniques on IEEE standard bus systems such as the 14, 30, and 118-bus models. For instance, Hernandez et al. demonstrated that metaheuristic-based allocation of FACTS improved reactive power distribution and minimized voltage deviation under varying loading conditions [96]. Similarly, Siddique and Adeli showed that advanced algorithms like GWO and HS could successfully balance power flows while enhancing reliability metrics [97]. The modern metaheuristic-based algorithms are particularly suitable for solving multi-objective power system optimization problems due to their global search capabilities and reduced computational effort as discussed in [98].

In conclusion, optimal placement and sizing of FACTS devices remain a critical area of research for enhancing the performance of modern power systems. The shift from traditional to metaheuristic and hybrid methods underscores the increasing complexity and dynamic nature of power grids. Future research should emphasize adaptive, AI-driven optimization frameworks capable of responding to real-time system conditions. With growing demands for grid flexibility and resilience, particularly in the face of renewable energy integration, the strategic deployment of FACTS devices will continue to play a pivotal role in sustainable grid evolution.

2.5 EV Integration in Power System Networks

Environmental concerns and the issue of global warming have already prompted governments to switch from fossil fuel cars to low-emission EVs. EVs are being developed in response to the energy crisis and environmental issues including air pollution and global warming. In recent years, one of the most important and exciting industries to develop is electric automobiles. Various reports claims that EVs are making an effort to displace more conventional, older cars. In addition to lowering emissions, these cars also save natural resources. As EV usage rises, the electrical distribution infrastructure has a number of power quality problems. As EVs become more prevalent in distribution networks, power quality problems such harmonic distortion, transformer failure, and voltage imbalance are predicted to occur. These problems are addressed by active power filters and FACTS devices, such as UPFC, dynamic voltage restorers, and parallel-series active power filters.

When high-frequency switches AC/DC functionalities are changed, power quality problems such neutral currents, reactive power needs, and THD rises. An EV battery charger is an apparatus which is used to charge electric cars. AC power is converted to DC to charge the batteries with the help of power electronic circuits which contains convertors. One crucial power electronic component that adds nonlinearity to the network and causes harmonic distortion of the electric grid side voltage or current is the battery charging mechanism of EVs [99]. Instability of a voltage in the electric grid can make the cost of voltage correction equipment increased. Switching losses in the AC-DC converters are also responsible for the power outage at the EV charging station. When EVs are integrated into the grid, the part of the system that is most susceptible to failure is the distribution transformer. An EV's harmonic level can vary from 3% at the beginning of charging to about 28% at the end [100-103].

2.5.1 Effects of EV charging on the distribution system

A voltage imbalance problem arises when the voltages in a three-phase power system have different magnitudes and phase angles (either too high or too low). This can be caused by a number of things, such as a city's home distribution network and the heavy reliance on single-phase loads, particularly in rural areas. Monte Carlo modelling has been used to assess how EV charging and discharging affect the voltage imbalance in a residential low voltage distribution grid since EV charging rates and connection locations are unpredictable [104]. EV charging stations, home battery storage, and single-phase photovoltaics can all cause an imbalance in the system voltage. Figure 2.3 shows the various issues caused with EV loading. The presence of negative sequence voltage components in power distribution systems with lengthy power lines causes a notable order of imbalance in the system's line current [105]. In a power circuit, low negative sequence impedance results in a voltage imbalance that is 6-10 times greater [106]. Therefore, excessive phase currents can shorten cable life, increase losses, cause additional heating effects, damage cable insulation, and trip overload protection circuits. These consequences include increased system vulnerability to failures (because an unbalanced system may not be able to feed loads efficiently) and decreased cable life [107]. Therefore, it is essential to detect and ascertain whether a circuit has voltage imbalance in order to address it promptly and guarantee that the power system and associated loads function properly.

Figure 2.3 Major power quality issues with the EV loading.

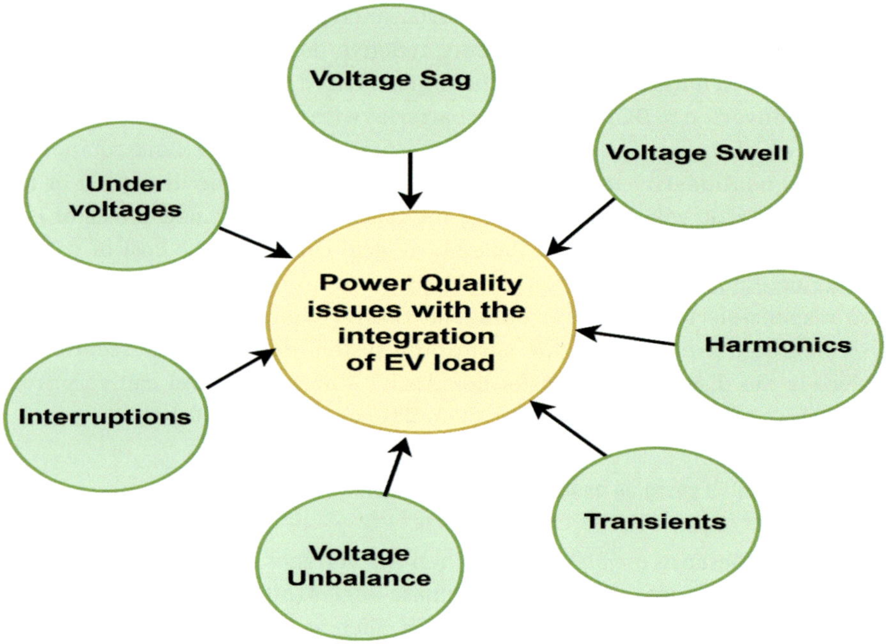

2.6 Research Gap

2.6.1 DG and FACTS are studied individually

Most existing research considers the optimal placement and sizing of DG or FACTS devices (like UPFC) separately. Their combined impact on techno-economic and operational performance of the power system remains underexplored.

2.6.2 Lack of coordinated optimization models

Very few studies develop a coordinated optimization framework that simultaneously integrates DG and FACTS devices to fully exploit their synergistic benefits on power loss reduction, voltage profile improvement, and cost minimization.

2.6.3 Limited application of multi-objective meta-heuristic techniques

Many studies rely on single-objective or conventional optimization methods, with insufficient use of advanced multi-objective metaheuristic algorithms like enhanced MOGWO, which are better suited for solving complex, multi-constraint power system problems.

2.6.4 EVCS load management is not jointly addressed with DG and FACTS

Although EVCS are recognized as a major emerging load, their impact is rarely managed using a combined DG and FACTS strategy. This leaves a gap in handling dynamic, high-demand scenarios in an optimal manner.

2.6.5 Inadequate scenario-based performance analysis

There is a lack of studies that evaluate the performance of DG and FACTS integration under realistic scenarios such as line outages, increased load conditions, or EVCS induced variability.

2.6.6 Limited comparative analysis between MODE and enhanced algorithms

Most works do not compare classical methods like multi-objective differential evolution (MODE) with enhanced algorithms like MOGWO under identical test conditions, which limits understanding of algorithm efficiency and robustness.

2.7 Conclusions

The review of existing literature and current practices in power system optimization clearly indicates that while considerable progress has been made in the individual deployment of DG and FACTS devices, their combined application remains insufficiently explored. Most studies do not address the simultaneous optimal sizing and placement of these components, thus failing to realize their full potential in improving system efficiency, stability, and economic performance. Moreover, conventional and single-objective optimization methods dominate the field, with limited application of advanced multi-objective metaheuristic techniques capable of handling complex, nonlinear, and multi-constraint problems in modern power systems.

Another significant gap lies in the area of EVCS load management, where dynamic and unpredictable demand patterns require robust, adaptive control strategies. However, the potential of using both DG and FACTS in a coordinated manner to address EVCS-induced stresses has not been adequately investigated.

Therefore, this book addresses these critical research gaps by proposing an integrated, multi-objective optimization framework that simultaneously optimizes DG and UPFC device deployment, effectively manages EVCS loads, and ensures improved technical and economic performance under various real-world scenarios. This comprehensive approach provides a practical foundation for developing intelligent, scalable, and future-ready power system networks.

CHAPTER

3

Multi-Objective Metaheuristic Optimization Techniques for Smart Grids

3.1 Introduction

In modern engineering systems, especially in power systems, optimization plays an important role in improving performance, minimising operational prices, improving efficiency, and maintaining reliability [108]. However, real-world optimization problems are rarely confined to a single objective. In most practical scenarios, decision-makers must consider multiple conflicting objectives simultaneously. For example, in a network, one might aim to reduce power losses while maximizing voltage stability or reduce generation cost while also minimizing emissions. These issues fall under the category of problems in which two or more objective need to be minimised, which are more complicated than single-objective ones by nature since they require the identification of a number of trade-off solutions as opposed to a single optimal point. Traditional mathematical and deterministic approaches often fall short in handling such complex, nonlinear, and non-convex problems, especially when the solution space is large, discontinuous, or poorly defined. This has led to the emergence of metaheuristic algorithms, which are nature-inspired, population-based, and stochastic optimization techniques capable of providing near-optimal solutions within reasonable computational times [109].

The incorporation of DG units, electric cars, and renewable energy sources has increased the complexity of power systems, necessitating the use of reliable and adaptable optimization techniques. Traditional deterministic approaches

DOI: 10.1201/9788743811176-3

often require gradient information and are sensitive to initial conditions, making them less suitable for solving real-world power system problems that involve discrete variables, nonlinear relationships, and conflicting objectives. In contrast, metaheuristic algorithms do not rely on gradient information and can efficiently navigate large and complex search spaces. When extended to the multi-objective domain, these algorithms are capable of generating a set of optimal solutions, known as the Pareto front, which provides valuable insights into the trade-offs among objectives. This is particularly useful in smart grid environments, where system planners must balance technical, economic, and environmental factors simultaneously. For instance, placing FACTS devices to improve voltage stability and power flow must also consider cost constraints, while optimizing EV charging infrastructure must balance energy availability, location convenience, and grid impact. By leveraging multi-objective metaheuristic algorithms, engineers and researchers can tackle such challenges effectively, making these algorithms indispensable tools in modern power system analysis and planning.

In recent years, a wide range of multi-objective metaheuristic algorithms such as Non-dominated Sorting Genetic Algorithm II (NSGA-II), MOPSO, and MOGWO have been developed and widely applied in various domains. These algorithms can efficiently explore the solution space and generate a diverse set of Pareto-optimal solutions, offering decision-makers the flexibility to choose according to specific preferences or constraints.

3.2 Need for Metaheuristic Algorithms

Real-world engineering problems, particularly in power systems, often involve multiple conflicting objectives, nonlinear behaviour, and complex constraints. In such scenarios, metaheuristic algorithms have emerged as powerful tools. Below are key reasons why metaheuristics are essential for solving multi-objective optimization problems.

3.2.1 Limitations of classical methods

Classical optimization techniques rely on mathematical models that assume continuity, differentiability, and convexity of objective functions. These assumptions often do not hold in real-world multi-objective problems, particularly in power systems where the solution space is nonlinear, constrained, and mixed with discrete and continuous variables. As a result, classical methods frequently fail to provide accurate or globally optimal solutions.

3.2.2 Handling discontinuities in the solution space

Many optimization problems involve discontinuities due to discrete variables or switching states. Such discontinuities result in undefined or non-differentiable objective functions. Metaheuristic algorithms, being derivative-free and stochastic in nature, can effectively explore these discontinuous and fragmented solution spaces.

3.2.3 Avoiding local optima

Multi-modal problems commonly contain multiple local optima. Gradient-based or local search methods tend to converge to the nearest local minimum, which may not be optimal. Metaheuristics incorporate mechanisms like randomness, mutation, and population diversity that enable global exploration and reduce the risk of premature convergence to local optima.

3.2.4 Managing combinatorial explosion

With increasing problem size and the presence of numerous decision variables, the solution space grows exponentially. This combinatorial complexity is difficult to manage using traditional exhaustive or enumerative approaches. Meta-heuristic algorithms utilize population-based or adaptive search strategies to explore vast search spaces efficiently without evaluating every possible combination.

3.2.5 Solving multiple objectives simultaneously

Multi-objective optimization involves finding solutions that balance trade-offs between conflicting goals. Metaheuristic algorithms are capable of identifying a diverse set of non-dominated solutions representing the Pareto front, allowing decision-makers to evaluate multiple optimal trade-off scenarios simultaneously.

3.2.6 Flexibility in constraint handling

Many real-world optimization problems include complex constraints, such as nonlinear equalities and inequalities, which are difficult to incorporate in traditional methods. Metaheuristics offer flexible constraint-handling techniques such as penalty functions, repair operators, and constraint dominance principles, enabling them to efficiently deal with constrained optimization problems.

3.2.7 Robustness and adaptability

Metaheuristic algorithms are robust across a wide range of problem types and scalable to larger problem instances. They perform consistently under varying problem conditions and can adapt to changes in the objective landscape or constraint structure without major reconfiguration.

3.2.8 Easy integration with other techniques

Metaheuristics can be integrated or hybridized with other optimization, machine learning, or decision-making techniques. This adaptability enhances their efficiency and allows them to be customized for domain-specific requirements or to improve convergence behaviour.

3.2.9 Capability to provide a set of solutions

Unlike deterministic methods that yield a single solution, multi-objective metaheuristics generate a set of optimal solutions in a single run. This feature enables a comprehensive exploration of the solution space and supports informed decision-making based on trade-off analysis.

3.3 Classification of Metaheuristic Optimization Algorithms

Metaheuristic algorithms can be grouped based on their source of inspiration into evolution-based, swarm-based, physics-based, and human-based categories as shown by Figure 3.1. Each category reflects a unique natural or behavioural phenomenon used to guide the optimization process.

3.3.1 Evolution-based algorithms

These algorithms are modelled after biological evolution and genetics. They work with a population of candidate solutions and improve them over generations using operators like selection, crossover, and mutation. Evolution-based algorithms are suitable for global optimization tasks in high-dimensional and complex landscapes.

3.3.1.1 Genetic algorithm

This algorithm is used in [110] to provide the best data for a load flow analysis. at order to put capacitor banks at key places along bus lines, the algorithm optimizes reactive power flow. It was tested on the Saudi Electricity Company (SEC) and switches between several load circumstances using a combinatorial technique. Similarly, the best location for BESS in a Virtual Power Plant (VPP) for distribution network planning was examined in [111]. While taking load increase and power output uncertainties into account, the GA was utilized to lessen power loss and power fluctuation brought on by PV plants.

3.3.1.2 Differential evolution

Another evolutionary algorithm, the DE, was created by Storn and Price [112] in order to improve performance, including rapid convergence. Target and difference vectors are created by the DE's operation, and they are then used to create trial vectors using the EA's traditional operators, such crossover and mutation. Both discrete and continuous variables may be handled by the DE thanks to this method [113]. In order to minimize energy losses in a meshed power network, [114] used the DE to determine the best locations, sizes, and power factors for DG units.

Figure 3.1 Classification of metaheuristic algorithms.

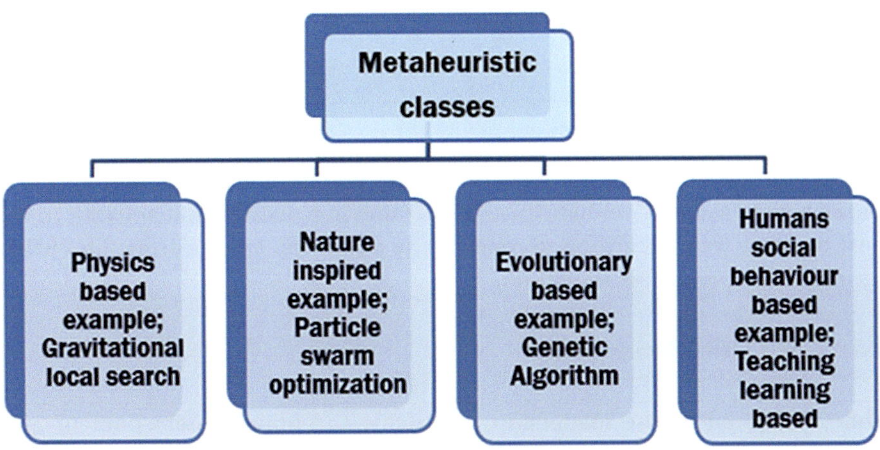

3.3.2 Swarm-based algorithms

This class of algorithms is focused on modelling how a swarm of animals (also known as search agents or particles) interact to accomplish a shared objective. The parameters that have the greatest impact on the algorithms' performance are included to the simulation. As a result, research on the best way to integrate electrical units has optimized and streamlined the number of parameters to increase grid performance by minimizing power loss and improving voltage stability. Swarm-based algorithms are widely used due to their simplicity and efficiency.

3.3.2.1 Particle swarm optimization

This algorithm models the social behaviour of birds or fish. Several PSO topologies were suggested in [115] for the best capacitor location, taking distribution system load patterns into account. Gaussian and Cauchy probabilistic distributions were used to generate random numbers in order to update the velocity equation, rather than a uniform probability distribution. Fifteen PSO mechanism types were produced by applying the distribution functions to the social and cognitive components in different ways. The PSO method was used in [116] to determine the best placements and sizes for DG units while taking into account harmonic power flow calculations for various harmonics based on nonlinear loads in a 31-bus distribution network. In order to maintain an appropriate degree of harmonic distortion, the authors analysed fuel, emissions, power loss, and the cost of DG units, in order to design and distribute the parallel capacitors in a radial power network as efficiently as possible as suggested by modified a PSO in [117].

3.3.2.2 Ant colony optimization

This algorithm mimics the pheromone trail following the behaviour of ants. By addressing power loss in addition to voltage variation and line loading, [118] shows how to use ABC to distribute BESS units in a distribution network in the best possible way. According to reports, the algorithm outperforms the PSO in terms of real power loss reduction.

3.3.2.3 Grey Wolf Optimizer

This is inspired by the leadership, hierarchy, and hunting behaviour of grey wolves in nature. This algorithm simulates alpha, beta, and delta wolves guiding the rest of the pack (omega) during the search process. It is known for its balance between exploration and exploitation and its success in engineering applications. The hybrid Grey Wolf Optimizer created by [119] doesn't require any parameter adjustment other than population size. This technique was used to decrease actual and reactive power loss in a distribution network by addressing the optimum DG allocation problem. Realistic limits were maintained for the bus voltages, DG unit sizes, and power factor on each bus.

3.3.3 Physics-based algorithms

These algorithms mimic physical processes such as gravity, motion, or thermodynamics and simulate the mechanisms of physical occurrences, which can be any natural event, chemical observations, or human interaction. Based on its mechanisms, this category can be categorized as an extension of swarm-based algorithms. One important difference between them is that physics-based algorithms can employ a single search agent to interact inside a solution search space, or vice versa, in place of a swarm of search agents.

3.3.3.1 Gravitational search algorithm

This simulates attraction among agents based on the gravitational forces. This algorithm was used to frame the optimal integration as a two-layer issue that maximizes the advantages of PV integration and minimizes yearly energy losses. The EV battery's status of charge was updated at each horizon and charge/discharge state according to the model. The first layer determines the best PV-DG unit placements and sizes based on EV charging and discharging power, and the second layer determines the best profiles for charging and discharging power [120].

3.3.3.2 Harmony search algorithm

This is another effective metaheuristic that relies on the pleasing arrangement of sounds. Reference [121] provides a thorough method, and [122] discusses in-depth about its application in enhancing power systems. In order to minimize the overall operating cost, reference [123] built this technique with some enhancement for the best possible unit integration in a distribution network.

3.3.4 Human-based algorithms

Based on human learning and behaviour, these algorithms simulate how people acquire knowledge or improve skills through interaction.

3.3.4.1 Teaching-learning-based optimization

This models the classroom learning process through teacher guidance and peer learning. To increase the stability of the grid while distributing the charging stations in IEEE 33 bus network, authors in [124] created a hybrid algorithm that combines TLBO with other techniques in a multi-objective space. The reliability index, power loss index, and voltage stability index make up the grid stability which reduces the possibility of an early convergence and speeds up convergence.

3.3.5 Comparison of single vs. multi-objective algorithms

- Single-objective algorithms are designed to optimize a single performance metric.
- Multi-objective metaheuristics (e.g., NSGA-II, MOPSO, MOGWO, MODE) handle two or more conflicting objectives and produce a Pareto front of trade-off solutions.
- Many algorithms, including GA, PSO, GWO, and DE, have been successfully extended into multi-objective variants to solve complex engineering problems involving multiple conflicting objectives.

3.4 Multi-Objective Optimization Problem (MOOP)

In mathematical terms, a multi-objective optimization problem can be generally expressed as follows [125] (assuming all objectives are to be minimized, without any loss of generality)

$$min Z(u) = \begin{bmatrix} Z_1(u) \\ Z_2(u) \\ \vdots \\ Z_k(u) \end{bmatrix}; u \in \Omega \tag{3.1}$$

where $\Omega = \{h(u) = 0, g(u) \leq 0\}$; Z, g, h are the vectors in which $Z : R^n \rightarrow R^k$, $h : R^n \rightarrow R^m$; $g : R^n \rightarrow R^{m1}$, u is considered as decision variable, k is number of objectives and m, $m1$ are equality and inequality constraints.

In real-world scenarios, it is not possible to find a solution that optimizes all k objectives at once. Consequently, multi-objective optimization problems are defined by a set of alternatives that are considered equivalent when there is no information about the importance of each objective compared to the others. These solutions are known as Pareto optimum solutions, which are synonymous with efficient, non-inferior, or non-dominated solutions. In objective space, the corresponding mapped points are commonly known as non-dominated solutions.

3.4.1 Pareto Optimal Solution (POS) definition

The vector $Z(\vec{u})$ is able to dominate another vector $Z(\overline{u})$ if and only if $Z_i(u) \leq Z_i(\overline{u})$ for all $i = \{1,2,3....k\}$ and $Z_j(u) < Z_j(\overline{u})$ for $j = \{1,2,...k\}$. Therefore, a solution

$u^* \in \Omega$ is considered as Pareto solution for multi-objective optimization problem if and only if there does not exist u $\in \Omega$ such that vector $Z(u)$ dominates another vector $Z(u^*)$.

Evolutionary algorithms are utilized to solve a number of practical issues and have attracted a lot of attention in the learning and optimization (single objective) fields. Various new evolutionary multi-objective optimization techniques have significantly expanded in the last 15 years. A collection of possible solutions is handled simultaneously by evolutionary algorithms. This feature enables the discovery of a whole set of Pareto optimum solutions in a single algorithmic run rather than requiring the execution of many distinct tuns, as is the case with conventional mathematical programming approaches. Furthermore, although mathematical programming approaches are concerned with the form and continuity of the Pareto front, evolutionary algorithms are less vulnerable to these two factors.

3.5 Multi-Objective Differential Evolution (MODE)

Storn and Price [112] in 1995 proposed the classical differential evolution (DE) algorithm for optimization problems. MODE is similar to the classical DE algorithm in which mutation plays a key role. In single-objective DE, the differential vector guides individuals towards the best solution, which is defined by the highest fitness value. However, this approach is incompatible with multi-objective optimization, where the aim is to find a set of Pareto optimal solutions representing trade-offs between conflicting objectives. Various election methods based on non-dominated sorting, crowding distance, or reference points can be employed to choose individuals for differential vector calculation. These modifications aim to balance the exploration of the solution space with the exploitation of promising regions, ultimately approximating the entire Pareto optimal set rather than converging to a single point. The challenge lies in maintaining the efficiency and simplicity of the original DE algorithm while adapting it to the complexities of multi-objective optimization.

3.5.1 Various steps involved in the MODE algorithm

3.5.1.1 Initialization of population

The MODE parameters, such as the maximum generation, number of decision variables, population size, mutation scaling factor, and cross-over frequency, are set during the first phase and creation of the initial population at random uses

$$A_{ij}^{u} = A_{min,i} + \left(A_{max,i} - A_{min,i}\right) * \alpha_{ij} \tag{3.2}$$

where $i = 1,2,...D$; $j = 1,2,3 .... N_p$, α_{ij} is a random number that varies between [0,1]. Superscript u is considered to be the iteration number and D is considered as decision variable. In this study, the power injected by the DG and UPFC and their locations were considered as decision variables.

3.5.1.2 Mutation process

The proposed MODE introduces a Pareto-based approach for selecting the best individual (P_{best}) in the mutation operation. This method identifies non-dominated solutions (D) at each generation, addressing the challenge of adapting DE to multi-objective optimization. For each individual (P), the algorithm determines if it is dominated or non-dominated to perform mutation operation. To find the dominated individual, a collection of non-dominated solutions can be identified that dominates this individual as shown by Figure 3.2. The best individual is then taken randomly from a collection of non-dominated solutions. The vector difference between P_{best} and P becomes the differential vector of this mutation operation. When the differential vector is 0, only perturbation vectors play an effect. Unlike single-objective DE, the best individual varies for each reproduction, aligning with the goal of finding the entire Pareto optimal set. Individual pairings from the parent population are chosen at random to define the perturbation vectors. The mutation operation may be expressed similarly to the single-objective DE after the differential vector and the perturbation vectors have been established.

The following equation is involved in the mutation process.

$$X_{j}^{u} = Y_{r1}^{u} + F\left(Y_{r2}^{u} - Y_{r3}^{u}\right) \tag{3.3}$$

where X_j^u is a mutant vector from randomly chosen vectors within the population, Y_{r1} is the best vector assigned for the base. The remaining two Y_{r2}, Y_{r2} vectors are assigned for the differential vectors, and F is the scaling vector.

3.5.1.3 Crossover process

This process enhances the variety of mutant parameter vectors and makes it easier for the algorithm to escape local optima. The crossover process at iteration (u) generates the trial vectors by mixing the parameters of the target vectors and mutant vectors according to a selected probability distribution.

$$V_j^u = \begin{cases} X_j^u, & if\left(rand(0,1) \le C_r\right) \\ W_j^u, & otherwise \end{cases} \tag{3.4}$$

Figure 3.2 A dominated solution in the current generation undergoes a mutation process and the differential vector is created.

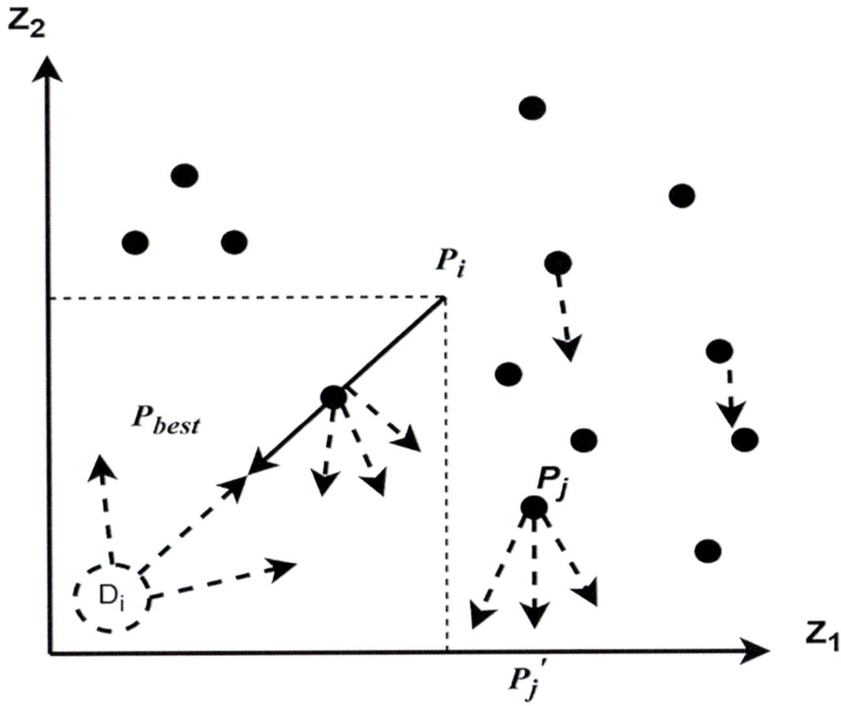

3.5.1.4 Pareto-based selection

By providing rank 1 to the non-dominated individuals and separating them from contention, this technique ranks the remaining non-dominated individuals in the population as rank 2, with the next highest fitness values, and so on, until every individual in the population has been assigned a rank. Each rank is given a so-called dummy value, with rank 1 containing the fitness value. Following each iteration's selection, the global Pareto solutions are updated, and a new population is added to the repository as shown in Figure 3.3. The following equation is used

$$A_j^{u+1} = \begin{cases} V_j^u \ \ if\, f\left(V_j^u\right) < f\left(A_j^u\right) \\ A_j^G \ \ if\, f(V_j^u > f\left(A_j^u\right) \\ A_j^k \Lambda \begin{cases} A_{N+m}^{u+1} = V_j^u \\ \Lambda \ m = m+1 \end{cases} \ else \end{cases} \tag{3.5}$$

where m is the natural number starting from 1 for each generation and N is the number of objective functions. Each generation's non-dominated solutions are selected from the respected generation's population and combined with the Pareto optimal set from the preceding generation.

Figure 3.3 Flowchart of MODE with Pareto solutions repository.

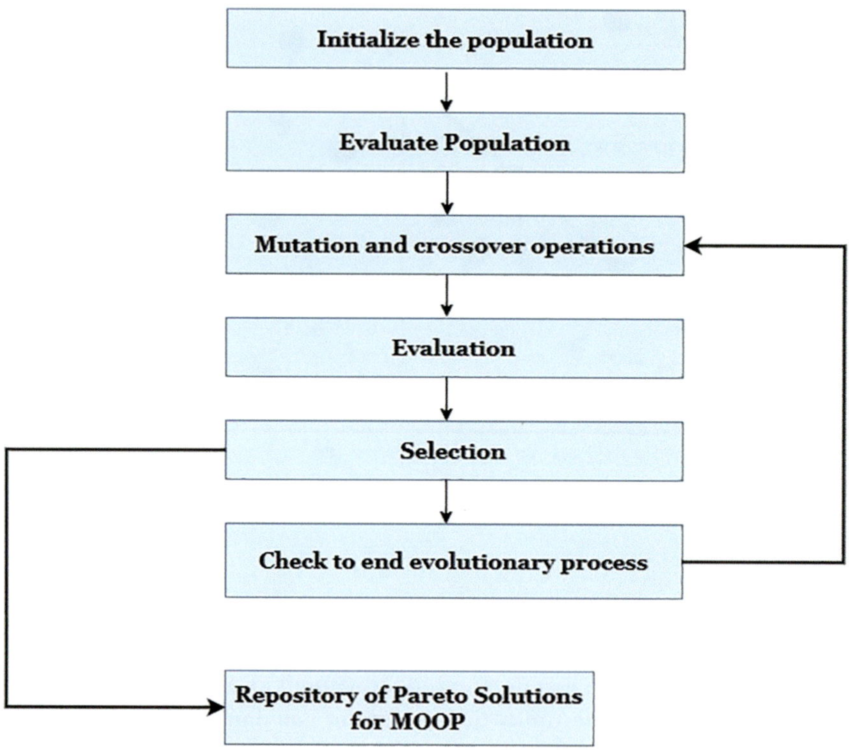

3.5.2 Pseudo code of MODE algorithm

NR load flow analysis is done to calculate base case power losses, voltage magnitude, line losses, and fuel cost.

To calculate total economic losses for the IEEE-30 bus system:

While $(iter \leq iter_{max})$

For $j = 1 : N_p$

Carry out mutation and crossover to generate trial vector (V_j^u)

If (V_j^u) crosses their boundaries

Re-initialize that population within their limits

end if

Calculate the fitness of newly generated trail vector (V_j^u)

If $f(V_j^u) < f(A_j^u)$

$A_j^{u+1} = V_j^u$

else $f\left(V_j^u\right) > f\left(A_j^G\right)$

$A_j^{u+1} = A_j^u$

else $A_j^{u+1} = A_j^u$

end for

solutions with previous iteration non-dominated solution set

output the best results

end

3.6 Improved Multi-Objective Grey Wolf Optimization (MOGWO)

3.6.1 Classical Grey Wolf Optimization

Mirjalili et al. introduced the grey wolf optimization algorithm as a novel swarm intelligence method in 2014 [126]. The leadership and hunting habits of grey wolves serve as the foundation for the grey wolf optimization algorithm. Wolves prefer to live in packs most of the time. The typical size of the group is between five and twelve, and there is a rigid dominating hierarchy. The alpha is the group leader and is in charge of choosing where to hunt, where to sleep, and when to wake up. The alpha wolf is sometimes referred to as the dominating wolf because the pack is expected to obey his or her commands. Even though they aren't the strongest, the alpha is the best at leading the pack. There is a beta after the alpha. It is the most qualified candidate to succeed the alpha in the event that the alpha dies or ages. It provides input to the alpha, serves as the pack's disciplinarian, and advises the alpha. The omega is the grey wolf with the lowest rating. The scapegoat role is what it performs. The term "delta" refers to wolves that are neither alpha, beta, or omega. They control the omega. This group includes guardians, hunters, elders, scouts, and sentinels [127]. The grey wolf's hierarchy is shown in Figure 3.4.

Figure 3.4 Hierarchy level in grey wolves' optimization.

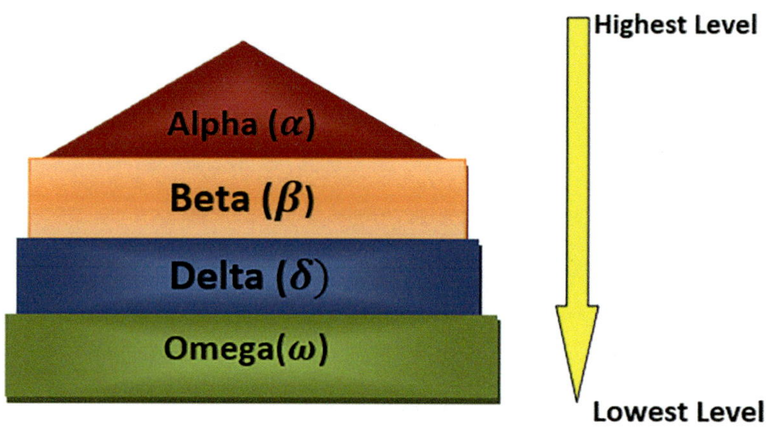

Alpha (α), beta (β), and delta (δ) are the best, second, and third, respectively, solutions in the GWO algorithm. It is believed that omega (ω) makes up the remainder of the answer. These three wolves are solely followed by the other wolves.

3.6.2 Oppositional-Based Learning concept (OBL)

In order to speed up reinforcement learning of optimization approaches in the field of computer intelligence, Tizhoosh in 2005 created opposition-based learning [128]. To have a better approximation for the candidate solution, it is based on the relationship between an estimate and its corresponding estimate. It is more likely to visit or even return to unproductive areas as a result. In comparison to both random and opposite-based solutions, the OBL solution has an even higher chance of reaching global optima. OBL is a novel machine learning approach that accelerates the convergence of several heuristic optimization methods. The use of OBL entails interpreting the existing and opposing populations in order to produce better candidate solutions for the given challenge within the same generation. In other words, when integrated with any optimizing technique it finds a fitter candidate solution from the beginning of the optimization process and uses opposing points to initialize the population and generation jumps.

3.6.3 Mathematical steps for the MOGWO algorithm

3.6.3.1 Initialization using OBL

This allows an algorithm to explore a wider range of probable solutions, potentially leading to faster convergence and improved optimization results. The incorporation of opposite points in the search space helps to diversify the initial population, reducing the likelihood of premature convergence to local optima. By leveraging both random and opposite-based initialization, OBL strikes a balance between exploration and exploitation, making it a powerful technique for enhancing the performance of metaheuristic algorithms like GWO. The following equation is used to randomly initialize each component.

$$A_i = A_{min,i} + rand(0,1)\left[A_{max,i} - A_{min,i}\right] \tag{3.6}$$

where $A_{max,i}$, $A_{min,i}$ are the maximum and minimum limits of the solution space, respectively, and Ai represents the current solution. Its corresponding oppositional matrix is formed as

$$\hat{A} = A_{max,i} + A_{min,i} - A_i \tag{3.7}$$

Here, A_i should be replaced by $\hat{A}$ if its fitness value is greater than that of A_i otherwise A_i should be used. Following initialization of the fittest population, the best fit is designated as α, the second best as β, and the third best as δ, depending on values.

3.6.3.2 Hunting

The following equations provides the mathematical model for surrounding the prey.

$$\begin{aligned} D &= \left|C \times A_p(u) - A(u)\right| \\ A(u+1) &= A_p(u) - Y \times D \end{aligned} \tag{3.8}$$

where k is the present iteration, A_p is the prey's position, A is the grey wolf location, and Y and C are the coefficients calculated as

$$Y = y \times (2r_1 - 1), \quad C = 2r_2 \tag{3.9}$$

where y decreases linearly from 2 to 0. Parameters r_1, r_2 were uniformly selected between [0, 1].

$$\begin{aligned} D_\alpha &= \left|C_1 \times A_\alpha - A(u)\right| \\ D_\beta &= \left|C_1 \times A_\beta - A(u)\right| \\ D_\delta &= \left|C_1 \times A_\delta - A(u)\right| \end{aligned} \tag{3.10}$$

where D is exploration parameter, C is tunning parameter randomly generated, and A is exploitation parameter.

$$A_p(t+1) = \frac{A_1 + A_2 + A_3}{3} \tag{3.11}$$

where A_1, A_2, A_3 are the optimal values of these three wolves in each iteration and the updated prey position is evaluated using above equation.

If $|\vec{A}| > 1$, then optimal candidate solution to find a fitter prey is away from the prey and if $|\vec{A}| < 1$, then the wolves are moving to the prey.

Following each iteration, α, β and δ, wolves adjust their positions as shown in Figure 3.5 to match the likely locations of the prey. Grey wolves attack their victim after it stops moving, completing the hunt. When every condition is met, MOGWO finally ends. All steps followed with GWO methodology is shown in Figure 3.6.

Figure 3.5 Schematic diagram of multi-objective grey wolf optimization.

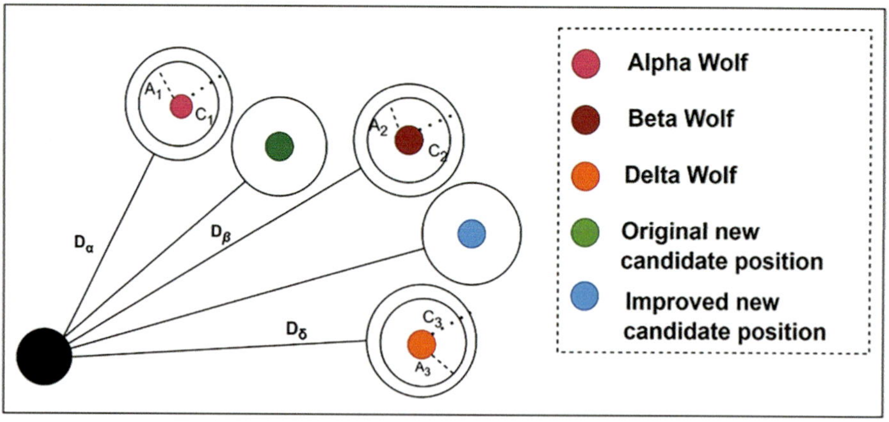

Figure 3.6 Flowchart for multi-objective grey wolf optimization.

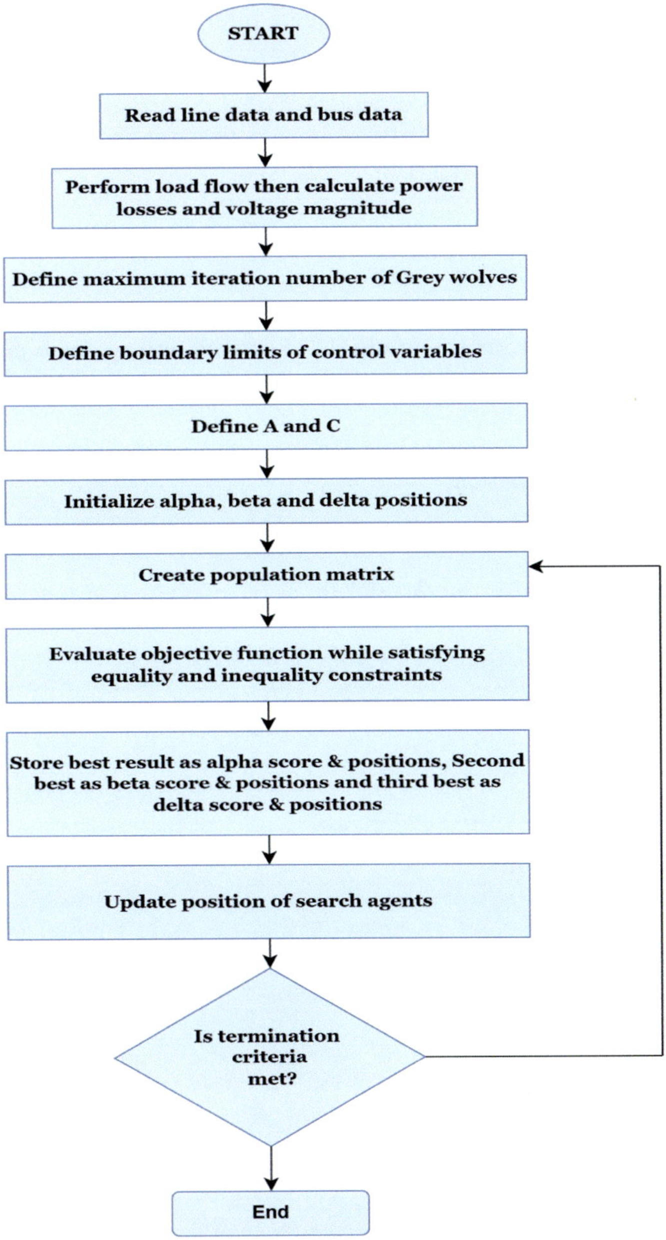

3.6.4 Pseudo code of MOGWO algorithm

Perform NR load flow analysis to calculate base case power losses, voltage magnitude, and line losses and then calculate total economic losses.

For $i = 1: D$

$j = 1: N_P$

$A_i = A_{min,i} + \text{rand}(0,1)[A_{max,i} - A_{min,i}]$

$\hat{A} = A_{max,i} + A_{min,i} - A_i$

end for

Select the fittest ones from the whole set of current and opposite populations by non-dominated sorting method and assign their corresponding ranks.

While $iter \leq iter_{max}$

for each wolf A_i in population

Calculate new position based on

$A(\alpha), A(\beta), A(\gamma)$ using $A(t+1) = \frac{A_1 + A_2 + A_3}{3}$

Evaluate new position's fitness

end for

Update α, β, γ

Calculate fitness of all search agents

Update $A(\alpha), A(\beta)$ and $A(\gamma)$

Update A_1, A_2, A_3

Update $\text{A}(\text{t}+1)$

$\text{t} = \text{t} + 1$

end

Select all non-dominated solutions by merging the entire solutions with previous iteration non-dominated solution set.

3.7 Conclusion

This chapter has provided a comprehensive overview of multi-objective metaheuristic optimization algorithms, emphasizing their growing significance in solving complex engineering problems, particularly within the power system domain. Traditional optimization techniques often fall short when faced with nonlinear, discontinuous, and multi-modal problems involving multiple conflicting objectives and a vast solution space. In contrast, metaheuristic algorithms, inspired by natural and social phenomena, have proven to be powerful alternatives due to their flexibility, robustness, and ability to discover globally optimal or near-optimal solutions without relying on gradient information. A structured classification of meta-heuristic algorithms was presented, including evolution-based, swarm-based, physics-based, and human-based approaches.

Among these, DE and GWO were identified as particularly promising due to their simplicity, fast convergence, and adaptability to multi-objective formulations. Their extensions, multi-objective differential evolution (MODE) and multi-objective GWO (MOGWO), were explored in detail to illustrate their working mechanisms, advantages, and relevance to real-world optimization tasks such as economic dispatch, DG and FACTS placement, and EVCS load management. By generating a diverse set of Pareto-optimal solutions, MOGWO and MODE offer system planners and engineer's valuable insights into the trade-offs between competing objectives. Their ability to maintain solution diversity, avoid premature convergence, and adapt to problem complexity makes them highly effective tools in modern decision-making environments. As power systems become increasingly integrated with renewable energy, DG, and intelligent infrastructure, the role of multi-objective metaheuristic algorithms will continue to grow in importance.

CHAPTER

4

Optimal DG Placement with EV Load in Smart Grids

4.1 Introduction

Electric Vehicle Charging Stations (EVCSs) are becoming increasingly essential in urban areas as the usage of EVs rises. This shift not only revolutionizes the transportation industry but also offers a significant chance to incorporate more renewable energy into the power supply. The introduction of EVs leads to a notable increase in electricity demand, which can be efficiently met by integrating renewable energy sources like PV and wind into the grid. This strategy not only aids in reducing carbon emissions from city transport but also tackles challenges such as air and noise pollution, decreases reliance on fossil fuels, and encourages innovative urban mobility solutions [129]. In several cities, renewable based DGs are a crucial component of their energy supply.

According to [130], more than 70% of qualifying cities make extensive use of solar, thermal, and solar photovoltaic technologies for power generation. Additionally, these cities are actively conducting feasibility studies and launching small-scale initiatives for local hydropower production. Some cities have already reached nearly complete reliance on renewable electricity, primarily sourced from hydropower and other renewable resources. Consequently, the integration of DGs with EVCSs offers cities a substantial chance to expedite their shift towards sustainable and emission-free urban settings. By combining renewable energy with electric transportation systems, cities can align with global objectives of reducing carbon emissions and enhancing urban living conditions.

DOI: 10.1201/9788743811176-4

However, literature [131-133] claims that power losses in the power networks account about 13% of the total electrical power. Furthermore, radial network's high resistance-to-reactance ratio results in higher voltage drop and power losses [134]. These deviations in voltages and power losses increase in instability with the growth in demand. Unusual operational conditions brought on by this spike in power consumption may provide stability and dependability issues for both utilities and customers. Both utilities and customers may face stability and reliability issues as a result of the typical operating conditions brought on by this spike in power demand. Therefore, the effective compensation is essential to address these issues and ensure that the power network operates safely and securely. Many researchers have employed techniques such as network reconfiguration, capacitor installation, and DG placement to minimize these losses and voltage deviation in distribution lines. Among these methods, DG placement is considered a prudent and effective option [135]. The literature extensively covers the planning of DGs. Reference [136] presents a multi-objective approach to determine best accommodation and size for multiple DGs, taking into account different load models. The issue of specifying DG penetration levels while adhering to voltage constraints is explored in [137–138]. Recently, optimization techniques that do not rely on gradients, such as GA, ACO, and PSO, have been employed to tackle these challenges [139–141]. Some research has highlighted that DG placement can enhance various operational conditions; for instance, [142] demonstrates that DGs can mitigate voltage drop issues, while [143] illustrates improvements in harmonics. Various methods were reviewed in [144] which are used in designing multi-objective strategies for DG placement, discussing challenges, future directions, and recent advancements. In [145], the ideal capacity and placement of DGs are considered, while proposing a non-separable and multi-objective optimization using the conventional dual method, which also includes harmonic distortion in the objective functions. Conversely, [146–147] focus on reducing the costs of DGs and system line losses. To boost the reliability and operational metrics of distribution networks, [148] proposes a hybrid planning approach that integrates DG planning with distribution automation, incorporating automated voltage-var control and automatic fault management. In order to balance the interests of DG owners, network operators, and consumers, a proper dynamic game-based bi-level synchronized planning of DGs and soft open points is presented in [149]. This allows for dynamic power changes between feeders.

Authors in [150] introduces a centralized and integrated objective function for DG planning in a regulated electricity system to identify the optimal mix of power plant and DG expansion, aiming to minimize decision-period costs related to generation expansion, maintenance, fuel, emissions, distribution losses, and anticipated energy not supplied. DG placement, along with the optimal placement, sizing, and management of battery energy storage systems, is presented in [151] as a mixed-integer non-linear programming model. Authors in [152] tackle the critical task of exploring the best placement of renewable DGs like PV, wind turbines, and EVs in the radial distribution system, a strategic move to reduce power loss and enhance the voltage profile and stability index. In [153], a combined approach using the voltage stability index and the marine predator's algorithm is proposed to address the allocation of DGs, shunt capacitors, and EVs in the distribution system. Reference [154] suggests an effective method to calculate the allocation problems of DGs and EV parking lots in the distribution system to decrease losses in the system and improve the voltage magnitude.

4.2 DG and its Types

DG is referred as the decentralized production of electricity by small-scale generating units that are located close to the point of consumers. Unlike conventional centralized power systems, which rely heavily on large power plants and extensive transmission networks, DG systems are connected to the distribution network or even directly to the consumer premises. This paradigm shift has gained momentum due to the growing demand for energy security, reliability, and sustainability, particularly in light of increasing integration of renewable energy sources. DG plays a crucial role in enhancing grid resilience, reducing transmission losses, deferring infrastructure investments, and facilitating the penetration of clean energy technologies [155–157]. The deployment of DG units enables the supply of active and reactive power locally, thereby alleviating stress on transmission lines and improving voltage profiles in distribution networks.

There are various types of DG technologies, broadly categorized based on their energy source and conversion technology as shown by Figure 4.1. One of the most prominent types is renewable-based DG, which includes solar PV systems, wind turbines, small hydro power plants, and biomass-based generators. Solar PV systems are widely adopted due to their modularity, low maintenance, and suitability for rooftop installations. Wind DG units, particularly small- and medium-sized wind turbines, are commonly used in rural and coastal areas with adequate wind resources. Biomass generators utilize organic waste or agricultural residues to produce electricity through combustion or gasification, offering an environmentally friendly alternative while managing waste.

Figure 4.1 Various types of DGs.

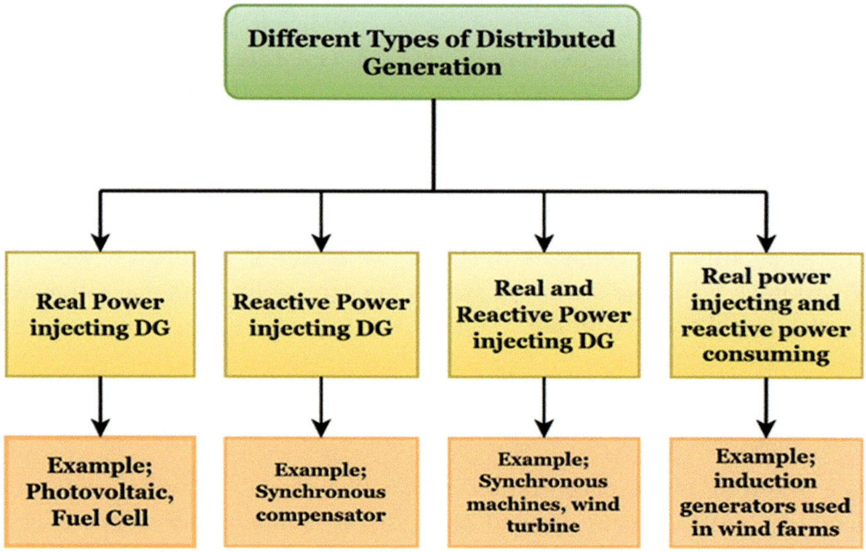

Another category includes non-renewable DG technologies, such as microturbines, gas turbines, diesel generators, and fuel cells. These systems, especially natural gas-fired units and combined heat and power (CHP) systems, are often employed in industrial and commercial sectors due to their reliability and capacity for cogeneration. Microturbines, which operate on natural gas or biofuels, are compact and suitable for distributed applications, offering high efficiency and low emissions. Fuel cells are an emerging technology that convert chemical energy from hydrogen into electricity with high efficiency and near-zero emissions, although they are currently limited by high costs and hydrogen infrastructure requirements.

Overall, the choice of DG technology depends on various factors including resource availability, load profile, regulatory framework, cost economics, and environmental considerations. With advancements in smart grid technologies and energy storage systems, DG is increasingly becoming a fundamental component of future power systems, contributing to a more resilient, efficient, and sustainable energy landscape.

4.2.1 Types of DG based on power output

DG units are classified into four major types based on their capability to deliver active power, reactive power, or both to the power system as presented in Table 4.1. This classification helps determine their role in voltage regulation, load sharing, and grid support services. The four types are as follows.

4.2.1.1 Type 1: DG Delivering Only Active Power

This type of DG is capable of delivering only active power (P) to the grid. These units do not supply reactive power (Q), and they often rely on inverters or converters for grid integration and power conditioning. Examples are PV systems, micro turbines, fuel cells. These sources typically generate DC, which must be converted to AC using power electronic converters. While modern inverters can be designed to supply reactive power, in conventional configurations these DGs primarily provide active power only.

4.2.1.2 Type 2: DG Delivering Only Reactive Power

This type of DG is designed to supply only reactive power (Q) to the system, without contributing to active power (P) generation. These units are typically used for voltage support and power factor correction, operating at a zero active power output. Examples are synchronous condensers, capacitor banks, and gas turbines (when run in synchronous condenser mode). Such DG units are especially beneficial in improving voltage profiles and maintaining system stability in areas with poor voltage regulation.

4.2.1.3 Type 3: DG Delivering Active Power but Consuming Reactive Power

DG units in this category are capable of delivering active power (P) to the grid, but they consume reactive power (Q) from the system to operate. This is due to the nature of their generator technology, primarily based on induction machines. Examples are induction generators used in wind energy systems (especially fixed-speed wind turbines). Induction generators do not have an internal source of excitation and hence draw reactive power from the grid. However, advanced configurations like Doubly Fed Induction Generators (DFIGs) can deliver both active and reactive power, making them more flexible.

Table 4.1 Various types of DG installed into a network.

DG Type	Delivers Active Power (P)	Delivers Reactive Power (Q)	Consumes Reactive Power (Q)	Examples
Type 1	Yes	No	No	PV, Fuel Cells, Micro turbines
Type 2	No	Yes	No	Capacitor Banks, Sync Condensers
Type 3	Yes	No	Yes	Induction Generators (Wind)
Type 4	Yes	Yes	No	Gas Turbines, CHP, Synchronous DG

4.2.1.4 Type 4: DG Delivering Both Active and Reactive Power

This type of DG is the most flexible and valuable in grid operation as it can simultaneously deliver both active (P) and reactive (Q) power. These units are usually based on synchronous generator technology, which allows precise control over both types of power output. Examples are Cogeneration units, gas turbines, and small hydro or biomass plants with synchronous generators. These DGs can be used not only for energy supply but also for voltage regulation, reactive power compensation, and frequency control, making them suitable for both grid-connected and islanded operation.

4.3 Multi-Objective Optimization Framework

This research focuses on formulating the multi-objective function which is used to improve the magnitude of voltage across buses and fuel cost of thermal power plants by minimizing the real power losses with optimization of DG smaller sizes.

$$F_{MO} = Min\{F_1(v), F_2(v), F_3(v), F_4\ (v)........F_n(v)\} \tag{4.1}$$

Subject to $h(v) = 0,\ \ g(v) \leq 0$

where F_{MO} is the multi-objective function, $h(v)$ is the constraint for equality and $g(v)$ is the constraint for inequality.

4.3.1 Objective functions

4.3.1.1 Minimizing power losses of system

This objective results in a decrease of power losses in MW. Equation 4.2 gives the illustration of function which provides a substantial reduction in the power losses.

$$F_1\left(P_{Loss}\right)=\sum_{\substack{m=1\\n\neq 1}}^{k}C_{PQ}\left(u_m^2+u_n^2-2u_mu_n\cos\left(\delta_m-\delta_n\right)\right) \tag{4.2}$$

where k is the total number of transmission lines, C_{PQ} is conductance between bus m and n, and δ_m, δ_n are the phase angle at m^{th}, n^{th} buses.

4.3.1.2 Minimizing DG operating price

The objective function for calculating DG total cost (F_2) is given as

$$F_2\left(DG_{T.C}\right)=C_{DG}\sum_{i=1}^{N}P_{DG} \tag{4.3}$$

where C_{DG} is the cost of power injected by DG's which has been taken 2 US$/Mw, P_{DG} is the total power generated from DG sources. The overall cost will be smaller with small capacity DGs.

4.3.1.3 Minimizing fuel cost of thermal generators

The objective function for fuel cost is given as

$$F_3(C_CG)=a_ip_i^{(2)}+b_ip_i+c \quad \text{US\$/h} \tag{4.4}$$

where C_{CG} is the fuel price function of conventional generators, p_i is the power in MW generated by i_{th} generator, a_i, b_i are the cost coefficients of the i_{th} generator.

4.3.2 Equality and inequality constraints

4.3.2.1 Voltage constraints

Voltage across each bus should be maintained within the prescribed limits. Therefore, the voltage is restricted with in a range given as

$$v_i^{min}\leq v_i\leq v_i^{max} \tag{4.5}$$

where i = 1,2,3...... 30 buses and voltage limits are between 0.95 and 1.08.

4.3.2.2 DG size limits

The relation effectively displays the limits of the DG size as

$$P_{min} \leq P_{DG} \leq P_{max} \tag{4.6}$$

where P_{min}, P_{max} is the minimum and maximum size taken for DGs, P_{DG} is active power from DG units.

4.3.2.3 Thermal limits

Thermal limit should not exceed up to

$$S_i \leq S_i^{max} \tag{4.7}$$

where i = 1, 2, n-1, n and S_i is the power in MVA at bus i.

4.4 Results and Discussion

Power flow simulations were performed using a range of DG units from 1 to 4 in MATLAB software to assess the feasibility and effectiveness of one or both MODE and MOGWO models. In order to analyse system behaviour, transmission line power losses, thermal power plant fuel costs, and DG operating costs are all taken into account at the same time. The IEEE 30-bus system is a commonly utilized model in power system analysis and control design due to its relatively small size, clear definition, and public accessibility. This makes it an excellent choice for evaluating and verifying new algorithms, techniques, and control strategies in the context of power system operations and planning. It consists of total number of buses 30, in which load buses are 24 and 6 are conventional generators located at buses 1, 2, 5, 8, 11 and 13. Table 4.2 shows a summary of 30 bus system, Table 4.3 gives the values of various parameters and Table 4.4 presents the values of control variables used for DG installation. Figure 4.2 shows the proposed methodology in steps.

Four cases were studied with both models:

Case 1: EV Load management with 1DG installed in a system

Case 2: EV Load management with 2DGs installed in a system

Case 3: EV Load management with 3DGs installed in a system

Case 4: EV Load management with 4DGs installed in a system

Table 4.2 Cost coefficients and generator limits of IEEE-30 for DG installation.

Bus no.	a (US$/MW²h)	b (US$/MWh)	C (US$/h)	P_{min} (MW)	P_{max} (MW)
1	0.00375	2	0	10	300
2	0.01750	1.75	0	10	100
5	0.062	1	0	10	150
8	0.008	3.25	0	10	55
11	0.025	3	0	10	30
13	0.025	3	0	10	40

Figure 4.2 Proposed methodology of MODE and MOGWO.

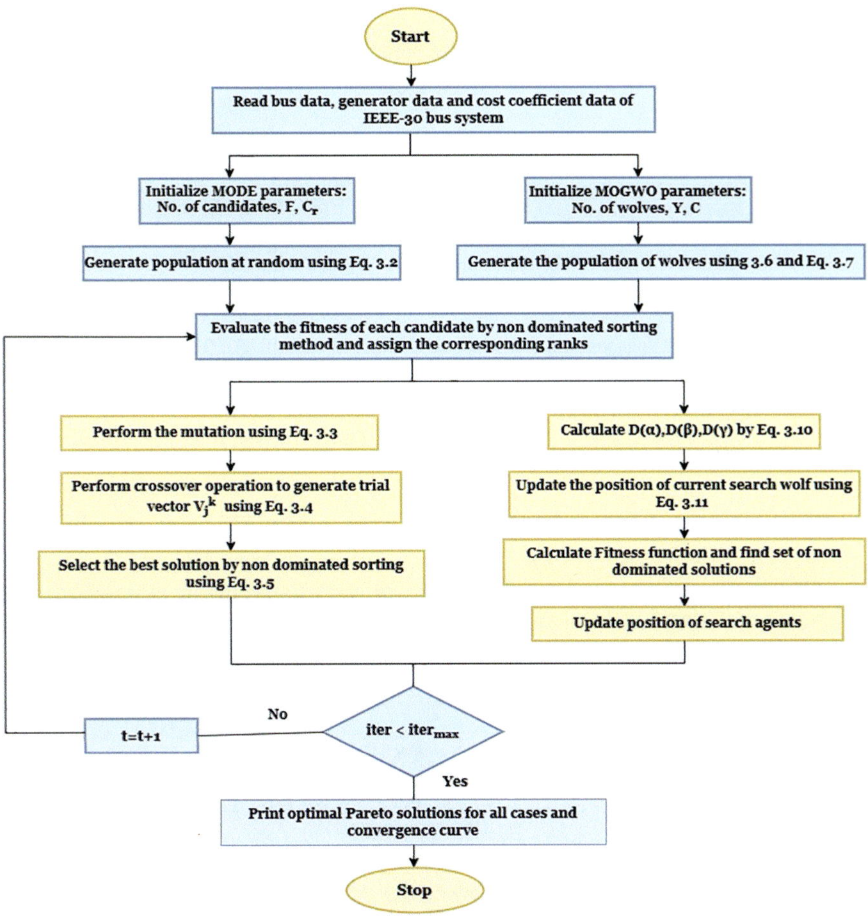

Table 4.3 Parameter setting values for DG installation.

Algorithm	Parameter	Value
MODE	Population size	50
	No. of iterations	100
	Crossover's Constant (C_r)	0.9
	Scaling Factor (F)	0.7
	Independent Runs	30
MOGWO	Number of wolves	50
	No. of iterations	100
	Coefficient Vector $\vec{x}$	[0,2]
	Random Vectors ($\vec{u}_1$, $\vec{u}_2$)	[0,1]
	Independent Runs	30

Table 4.4 Control variables settings for DG installation.

Variable	Range
DG_{Size}	[10,300]
X_F	[–0.2, 0.8]
V_{VR}	[0.9, 1.05]
V_{CR}	[0.9, 1.05]
δ_{VR}	[0, π]
δ_{CR}	[0, π]
Generator Voltages	[0.98,1.08]
Transformer taps	[0.9, 1]
Shunt Capacitors (Q_{SH})	[0, 0.15]
Reactive generation (*MVar*)	[–50, 100]

The total economic loss (TEL) for the system with EV loads, which results from the DG placement adding extra load and losses with DG, is added in the DG's TEL, whereas the energy loss from power distribution expenditures is reflected in the TEL without DG. Therefore, the difference between $TEL_{withoutDGs}$ and $TEL_{withDGs}$ shows the total cost savings due to Optimal DG Placement for the system managing EV loads (ODGPEVs).

$$\mathrm{TEL_{withoutDGs}} = \left[\mathrm{P_{losseswithoutDG}} \times \mathrm{C_e} \times 8760 \times 1000\right] \mathrm{US\$} \tag{4.8}$$

where C_e is the cost of energy due to losses 0.05 US$/Mw

$$\mathrm{TEL_{withDGs}} = \left[\mathrm{P_{losseswithDG}} \times \mathrm{C_e} \times 8760 \times 1000 + \frac{\mathrm{C_{DG}} \sum_{i=1}^{N} \mathrm{P_{DG}}}{\mathrm{L_{DG}}}\right] \mathrm{US\$} \tag{4.9}$$

where L_{DG} is the life of DG taken as 10 years

Therefore, to calculate the benefits of placing DG optimally into the system can be calculated as

$$\text{Total Savings} = \left[\text{TEL}_{\text{withoutDGs}} - \text{TEL}_{\text{withDGs}}\right] \text{ US\$} \tag{4.10}$$

To examine network performance with various parameter setting values and boundary limits of control variables are given in Tables 4.4 and 4.5.

4.4.1 Multi-objective power flow analysis for ODGPEVs

Under normal loading scenarios, an IEEE-30 bus system has a total load of 283.4 MW and 126.2 MVar. The N-R load flow analysis reveals losses of 17.55 MW in real power and 67.69 MVar in reactive power, based on a 100 MVA base case. In this scenario, the total power generation reaches to 300.9 MW, with Generator 1 contributing 260.96 MW and Generator 2 supplying 40 MW. When loading is increased due to addition of EVCS into the system at load buses 10, 12, 14, 16 and 17 where buses were selected on the basis of minimum amount of voltage variations. Besides these charging stations, 7.2 KW load is also added to each bus, so that consumer can charge their vehicle at home also. Therefore, the total load rises to 301.59 MW with power losses increases to 19.97 MW and power generation becomes 321.52 MW and the fuel cost become 958.24 US$/h for the base case. TEL for the base case becomes 7.687×10^6 US$.

A modified optimal power flow with MODE and MOGWO techniques has been run to find optimal locations and sizes of DGs so that total power losses and fuel costs can be minimised.

Figure 4.3 shows the power losses over 41 branches in a system before and after optimization with DG configurations for MODE and MOGWO. With a notable loss at branches 1, 2, and 5, shown by the red line, represents the state "Before Optimization," displays the biggest power losses across all branches. After optimization, power loss significantly decreases across the branches, as depicted by other coloured lines. The configuration incorporating 3DG and 4DG units shows more steady and minimum power losses across most branches, and Figure 4.4 illustrates the total loss reduction. It is clear that increasing the number of RDG units and using these optimization procedures consistently reduces power losses.

Figure 4.5 shows the Pareto optimal solutions for the IEEE 30-bus system, when DGs were varied from 1 to 4 units. The convergence characteristics MODE and MOGWO algorithm is presented in Figure 4.6. Table 4.8 shows that the power losses with 1DG placement were reported to 6.88 MW and 6.89 MW using MOGWO and MODE, respectively. When 2DGs were installed for managing EV load, power losses with MOGWO and MODE were 5.35 MW and 5.83 MW, respectively. Power losses were lowered to 4.49 MW and 5.01 MW with MOGWO and MODE when 3DGs was installed. Finally, these losses with 4DGs amount to 4.09 MW with MOGWO and 5.05 MW with MODE technique.

Figure 4.3 Line losses improvement in IEEE-30 bus system.

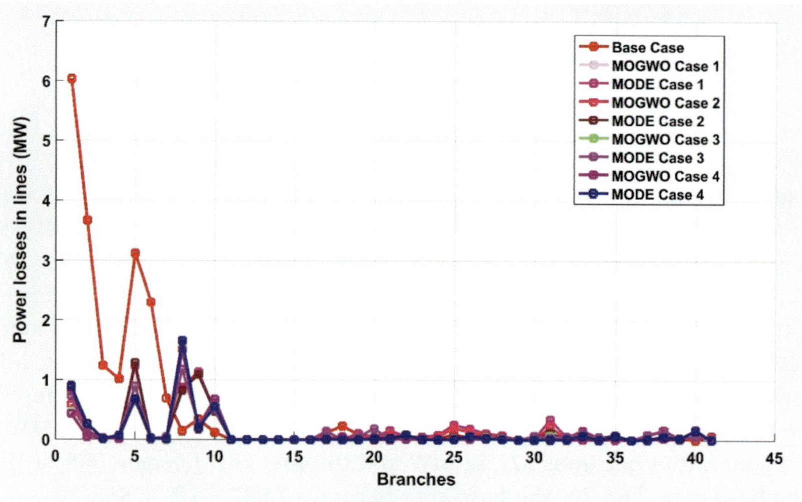

Figure 4.4 Total power losses reduction in IEEE-30 bus system for all cases.

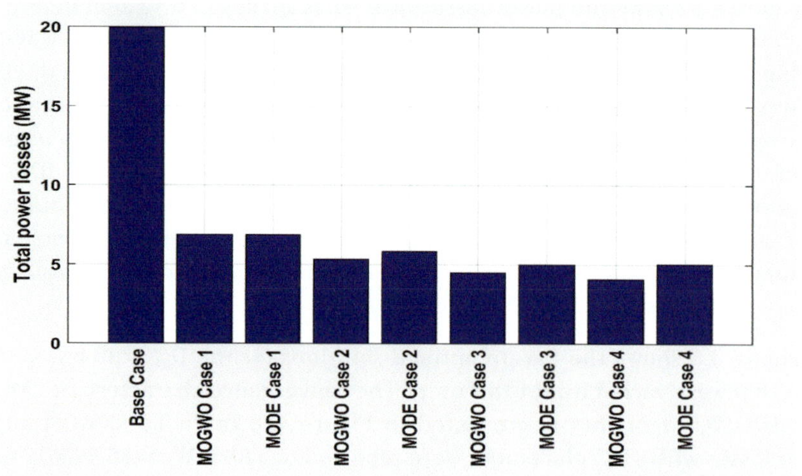

Figure 4.5 Non dominated solutions for EV loading: (a, b) with 1DG; (c, d) with 2DGs; (e, f) with 3DGs; (g, h) with 4DGs.

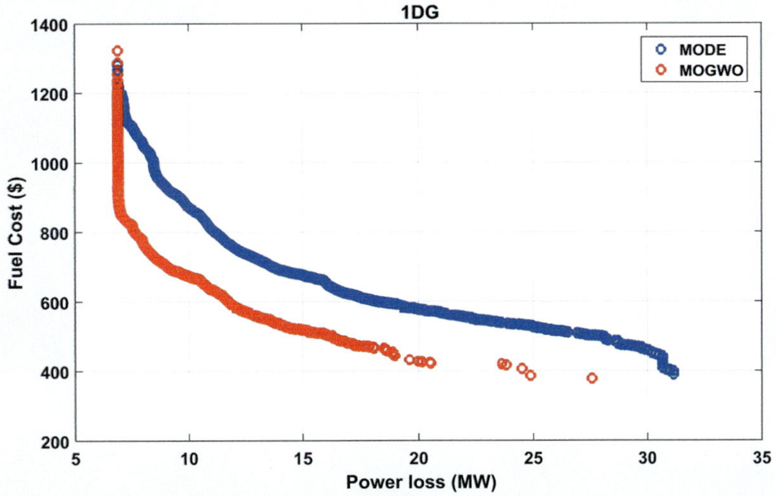

(a)

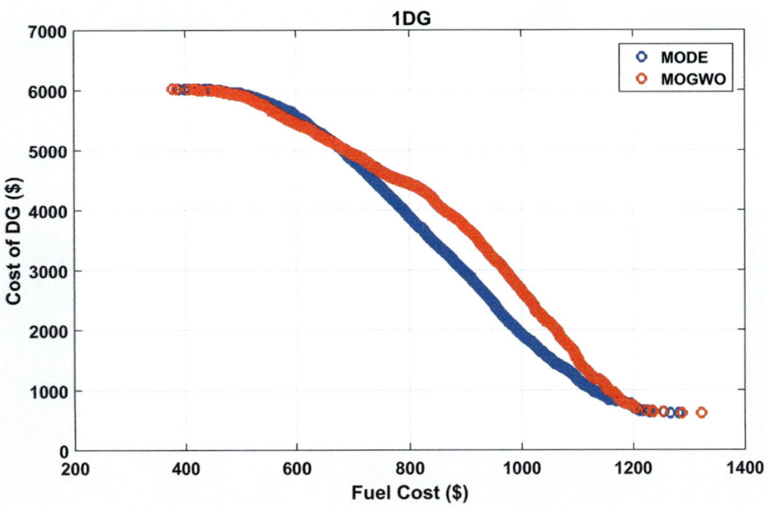

(b)

(*Continued*)

Figure 4.5 *Continued*

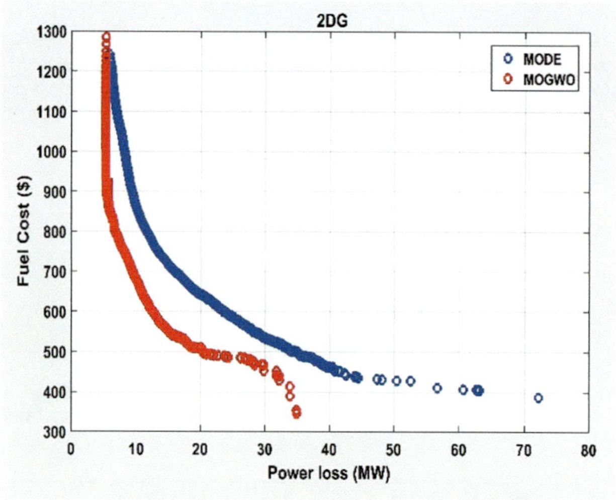

(c)

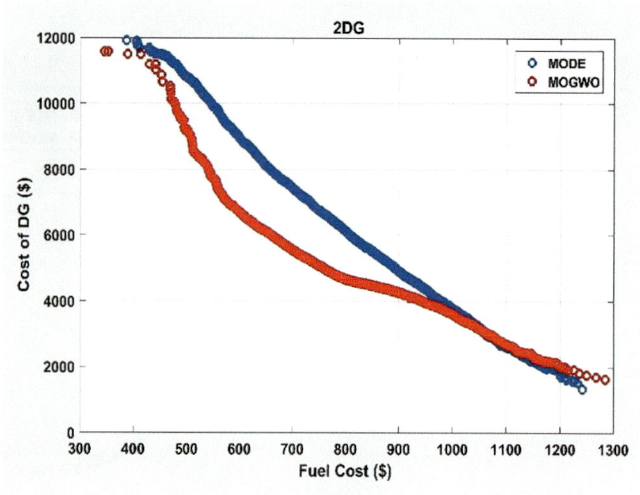

(d)

Figure 4.5 *Continued*

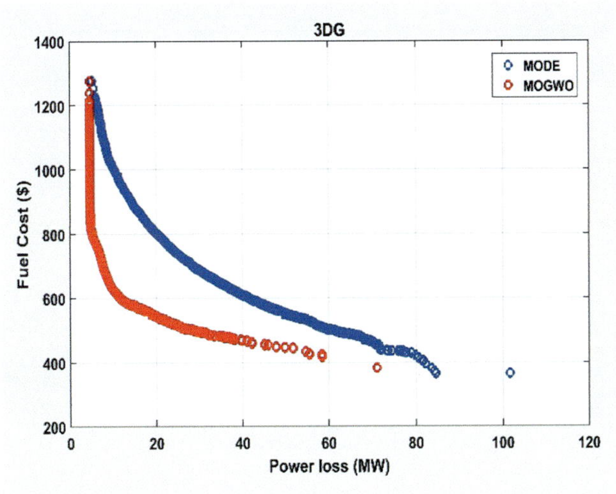

(e)

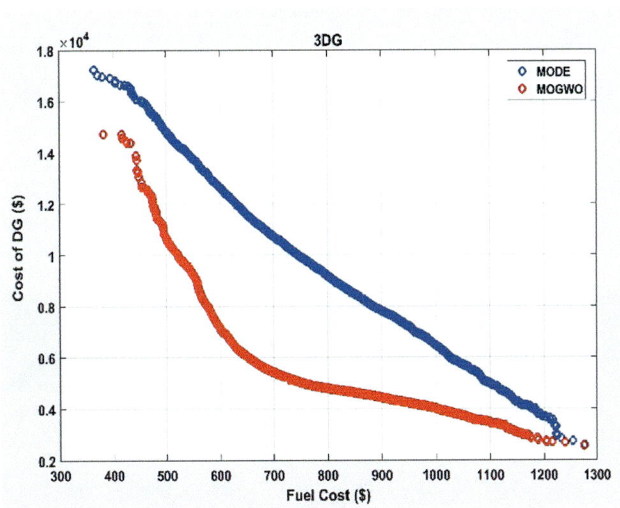

(f)

(*Continued*)

Figure 4.5 *Continued*

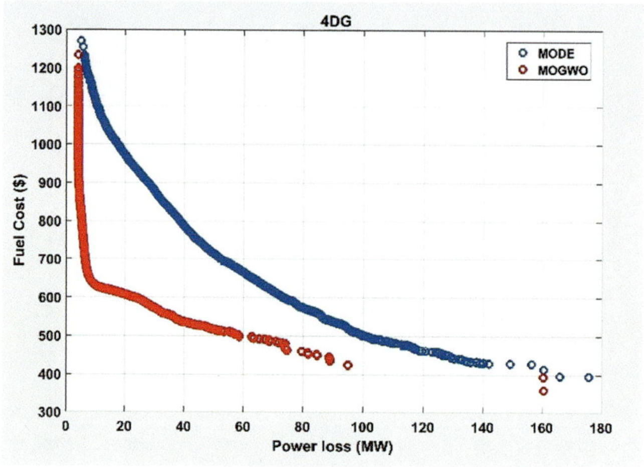

(g)

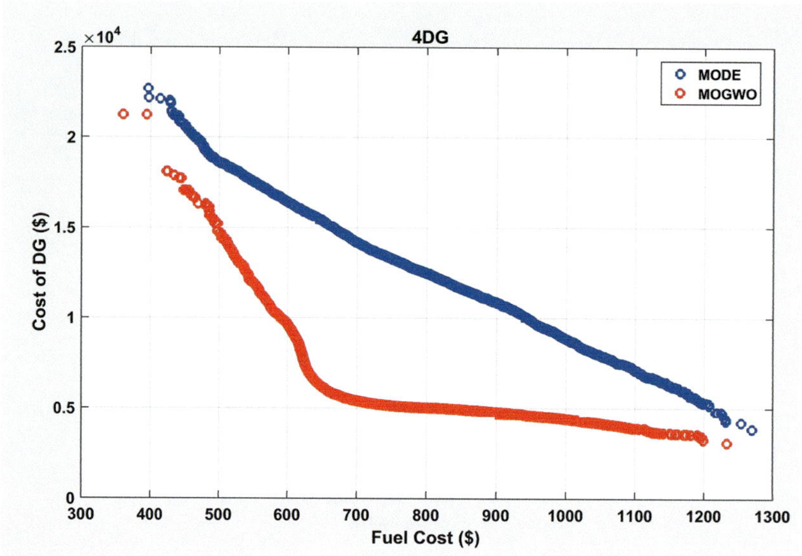

(h)

Table 4.5 Optimum scheduling of fuel generators for IEEE-30 under MODE techniques.

Case	P_{G1} (Mw)	P_{G2} (Mw)	P_{G5} (Mw)	P_{G8} (Mw)	P_{G11} (Mw)	P_{G13} (Mw)
1	164.98	75.57	28.98	32.75	18.72	31.45
2	98	47	20	26	27	15
3	75	36	48	14	19	31
4	154	46	18	16	20	38

Table 4.6 Optimum scheduling of fuel generators for IEEE-30 under MOGWO technique.

Case	P_{G1} (Mw)	P_{G2} (Mw)	P_{G5} (Mw)	P_{G8} (Mw)	P_{G11} (Mw)	P_{G13} (Mw)
1	70	56	50	23	25	40
2	115	52	42	17	21	29
3	152	33	23	25	19	27
4	75	55	29	19	23	21

Table 4.7 Reactive power losses in lines without and with DG for EV loading.

Line no.	Base Case	MODE (case 4)	MOGWO (case 4)	Line no.	Base Case	MODE (case 4)	MOGWO (case 4)
1	18.074	2.699	1.288	**19**	0.184	0.001	0.0157
2	13.405	0.964	0.159	**20**	0.001	0.015	0.025
3	3.775	0.042	0.065	**21**	0.013	0.080	0.015
5	13.09	2.857	2.860	**24**	0.037	0.002	0.006
6	6.962	0.076	0.067	**25**	0.195	0.023	0.045
7	2.411	0.034	0.007	**26**	0.097	0.160	0.097
8	0.356	4.184	3.801	**27**	0.234	0.053	0.046
9	1.037	0.587	0.647	**28**	0.105	0.024	0.019
10	0.417	1.943	2.372	**29**	0.001	0.002	0.006
17	0.241	0.241	0.005	**31**	0.063	0.028	0.008
18	0.451	0.451	0.085	**37**	0.163	0.026	0.009

Table 4.8 indicates that the MOGWO strategy produced the lowest generating cost and power losses when 4DGs were installed. After installing 4DGs, the MOGWO and MODE approaches resulted in considerable cost reductions of 76.91% and 71.23%, respectively. When the generator cost, DG size, and power losses are all adjusted at the same time, the voltage profile is also enhanced with 4DGs. It is found that the MODE technique reduces the size of multi-DGs. Consequently, the MODE technique is determined to have a lower cost for DGs. Although the MOGWO technique is more expensive than the MODE approach

for DGs when four DGs are deployed, power loss mitigation is prioritized during heavy loading situations. Consequently, in this case, the MOGWO strategy is thought to be superior to the MODE approach.

Table 4.8 Result summary of optimal power flow output with DG only under both models.

No. of DGs	Method	DGs Optimal Sitting/ Size (MW)	Power Losses (MW)	Fuel Cost (US$/h)	DG Cost (US$)	TEL_{DG} (US$)
1	MODE	9/224	6.89	1046.52	4480	3.018×10^6
	MOGWO	9/224	6.88	847.51	4480	3.014×10^6
2	MODE	9/157; 15/64	5.83	638.36	4420	2.554×10^6
	MOGWO	9/163; 7/70	5.35	810.52	4660	2.343×10^6
3	MODE	7/45; 9/99;14/87	5.01	679.23	4620	2.194×10^6
	MOGWO	7/63; 9/119;15/64	4.49	776.35	4920	1.967×10^6
4	MODE	7/84;10/60; 18/31;30/36	5.05	828.12	4220	2.212×10^6
	MOGWO	7/58;9/100; 15/62; 30/30	**4.09**	**623.12**	**5000**	$\mathbf{1.791 \times 10^6}$

The voltage profile across 30 buses is shown by Figure 4.7 both before and after optimization with various DG units utilizing the MODE and MOGWO algorithms. Significant voltage drops are seen by the red line, which represents the voltage "Before Optimization," with values frequently falling below 1 pu, particularly at buses 26 and 30. On the other hand, there are noticeable gains in the magnitude of voltage when employing different DG integrations. MODE with 4DG maintains the most stable and high voltage profile, coming in close to 1.08 pu, demonstrating its ability to stabilize voltage levels throughout the system.

Voltage magnitude is also enhanced with 2DG or 3DG configurations under MODE and MOGWO but not as much enhanced as with 4DG under MODE technique. A comparison of several configuration (cases) under both algorithms for power system performance, with an objective to reduce fuel cost and power loss, is provided in Table 4.8. Consequently, the outcomes demonstrate the MOGWO's efficacy in comparison to other well-established techniques. The MOGWO algorithm is the most efficient method, achieving the lowest power loss of 4.09 MW and a fuel cost of US$ 623.12/hr. Therefore, the capacity of MOGWO to handle multi-objective optimization problems in power flow studies is demonstrated by its excellent result.

Figure 4.6 Convergence characteristics of MODE and MOGWO for different DG configurations.

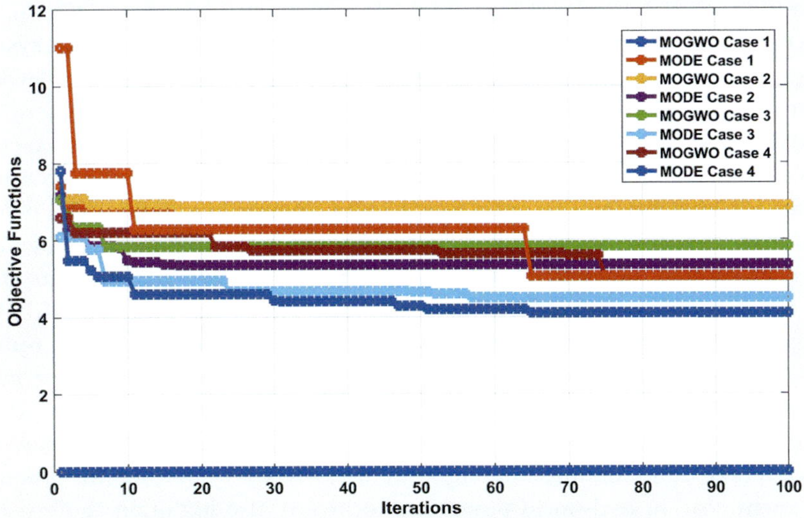

Figure 4.7 Bus voltage improvement with DG integration only.

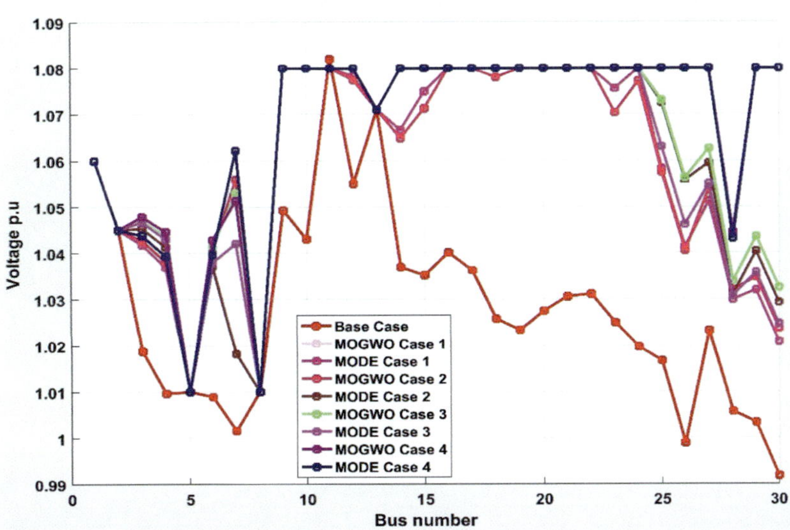

4.5 Conclusion

A significant improvement in system performance was observed after the integration of DG units. The optimal placement and sizing of DGs led to reduced power losses, improved voltage profiles, and enhanced overall system efficiency. When coupled with an advanced optimization method like MOGWO, the presence of DGs further amplified the benefits, highlighting a synergistic effect. DG installation contributed not only to technical enhancement such as reduced transmission losses and better load balancing but also to economic advantages by lowering the operational cost of power generation. The results emphasize the crucial role of DGs in modern power systems, especially under increasing demand scenarios. Furthermore, they demonstrate that the combination of DG with powerful optimization techniques like MOGWO can significantly optimize power flow, improve grid reliability, and reduce operational expenditures. This integrated approach paves the way for more resilient, efficient, and economically viable power networks, particularly in the context of evolving grid challenges and the integration of renewable energy sources. The findings not only validate MOGWO's potential for practical implementation in real-world power networks but also highlight the growing importance of metaheuristic algorithms in achieving operational excellence. These results can guide future research towards hybrid models, real-time optimization frameworks, and the inclusion of renewable generation sources within the optimization process.

CHAPTER

5

Co-Optimization of DG and FACTS Devices for EV-Integrated Smart Grids

5.1 Introduction

The accelerating adoption of EVs is playing a transformative role in the global transition toward sustainable and low-carbon transportation systems. This rapid growth, while beneficial from an environmental standpoint, presents significant challenges to existing power system infrastructure, particularly in terms of EVCS. The aggregated and often uncoordinated charging demand from EVCS can cause substantial stress on the power distribution network, leading to voltage fluctuations, increased peak loads, network congestion, and reliability issues. In this context, effective load management strategies for EVCS have become essential to ensure the stability and efficiency of power system operations. Traditional grid-centric solutions are often inadequate in addressing the dynamic and localized nature of EV charging loads. Therefore, integrating renewable DG sources, such as solar photovoltaics and wind turbines located in proximity to EVCS, offers a promising pathway for reducing the burden on the central grid. These sources can provide localized energy support, reduce peak demand, and enhance energy resilience.

However, the variable and intermittent nature of renewable DGs introduces new complexities in terms of voltage regulation, frequency stability, and real-time power balancing. To address these challenges, advanced power electronics-based compensation devices, particularly the UPFC, are increasingly being explored. The UPFC, a member of the FACTS family, is capable of simultaneously

DOI: 10.1201/9788743811176-5

regulating voltage magnitude, controlling line power flow, and improving power quality by controlling both active and reactive power. By dynamically adjusting power flow paths and voltage profiles, the UPFC can help accommodate fluctuating renewable generation and variable EVCS loads effectively.

The coordinated integration of renewable DG sources and the UPFC controller presents a robust solution for EVCS load management. Such an approach can optimize grid performance by minimizing power losses, enhancing voltage stability, reducing dependency on fossil-fuel-based generation, and facilitating higher penetration of EVs and renewables. Furthermore, it enables economic benefits through reduced energy costs, deferred infrastructure investments, and improved utilization of local generation assets.

In [158], the authors enhanced system loadability using different FACTS devices optimized through the ABC algorithm, further contributing to the stability of the power network. The FFO algorithm, along with FACTS devices for power transmission fault analysis, show notable results in fault detection and system reliability [159]. The YYPO technique [160] for electrical network security enhancement using FACTS indicates substantial improvements in system security with the implementation of the STATCOM, UPFC, and IPFC controllers. A MLAPO approach for the best positioning of FACTS devices effectively improves network performance [161]. The ASO algorithm for security enhancement in power systems, underlining its potential in optimizing FACTS device placement, was developed by [162]. The authors of [163] focused on enhancing power network security through a multi-objective technique to determine the location and size of the SVC. In [164], the author addressed contingency management through the optimal reallocation of generators using the TCSC, highlighting practical implications for power system operations. The PSO technique was applied to the IEEE-14 bus system to obtain the optimal reactive power dispatch [165]. Reactive power planning is performed using FACTS controllers such as SVC and TCSC [166]. Hybridization of the Grey Wolf Optimizer and Particle Swarm Optimization is applied to the IEEE-14, 30, and 118 bus systems to minimize power losses and voltage deviation [167]. FACTS controllers minimize the power losses and fuel cost using the multi-objective flow direction algorithm in [168] and with the Moth-Flame Optimizer (MFO), Barnacles Mating Optimizer (BMO), and TLBO techniques in [169]. Twelve proton exchange membrane fuel cells were successfully optimized in [170] using a depth information based differential evolution technique, which facilitated the expansion of PEMFC utilization in clean energy applications.

This chapter focuses on developing a comprehensive framework for EVCS load management using renewable DG sources in conjunction with a UPFC controller. It aims to evaluate the technical and economic performance of a distribution network under various scenarios, including peak EV charging periods, fluctuating renewable output, and varying UPFC control strategies. Load flow analysis, voltage profile monitoring, and optimization algorithms are employed to determine the optimal location and size of DG and UPFC units for improved network efficiency.

5.2 Modelling of a UPFC Controller

The concept of UPFC was introduced by Gyugyi [171] in 1991. It can maintain the voltage and power flow through a transmission line. The purpose of UPFC is to monitor and control the voltage, phase angle, and reactance of the line. There are two possible control modes for the UPFC. The first is the VAR-control mode and the other is the automatic voltage control mode. As shown in Figure 5.1, two converters are used in this device. One was connected in a shunt, and the second was connected in series. The job of the first converter is to maintain the voltage for the second converter. A series converter regulates both the actual and reactive powers within the branch lines. The shunt converter maintains a constant voltage for the DC bus.

Figure 5.1 Static model of UPFC controller.

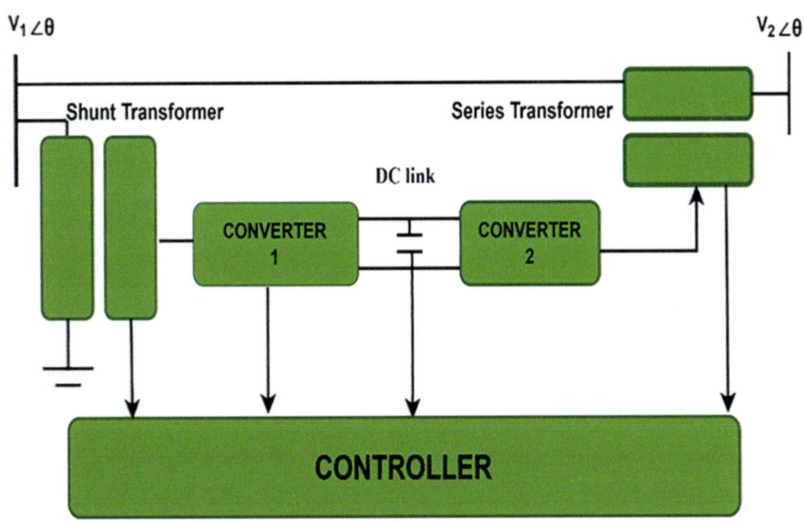

The shunt converter is STATCOM and the second is SSSC in unified power-flow controller devices. Another important function of this controller is to reduce the power oscillations in the system. There is one major limitation in that it works only on balanced sinusoidal waves. This controller can be installed at any position on the transmission line and can be connected at the sending end of the system, in the receiving end of the system, or in the middle of the transmission line. The operation of UPFC angle is from $-\angle 180$ to $+\angle 180$. The voltage equations for two series and shunt source convertors are described as:

$$E_{VR} = V_{VR}\left(\cos\delta_{VR} + \mathrm{I}\,\sin\delta_{VR}\right) \tag{5.1}$$

$$E_{CR} = V_{CR}\left(\cos\delta_{CR} + i\,sin\delta_{CR}\right) \tag{5.2}$$

The actual and reactive power equations are described as:

$$\begin{aligned} P_m = {} & V_m^2 G_{mm} + V_m V_n \left(G_{mn}\cos(\theta_m - \delta_n) + B_{mn}\sin(\theta_m - \delta_n)\right) \\ & + V_m V_{CR}\left(G_{mn}\cos(\theta_m - \delta_n) + B_{mn}\sin(\theta_m - \delta_n)\right) \\ & + V_m V_{CR}\left(G_{VR}\cos(\theta_m - \delta_n) + B_{VR}\sin(\theta_m - \delta_n)\right) \end{aligned} \tag{5.3}$$

$$\begin{aligned} Q_m = {} & -V_m^2 B_{mm} + V_m V_n \left(G_{mn}\cos(\theta_m - \delta_n) - B_{mn}\right) \\ & + V_m V_{CR}\left(G_{mn}\cos(\theta_m - \delta_n) - B_{mn}\sin(\theta_m - \delta_n)\right) \\ & + V_m V_{CR}\left(G_{VR}\cos(\theta_m - \delta_n) - B_{VR}\sin(\theta_m - \delta_n)\right) \end{aligned} \tag{5.4}$$

where, V_{CR} and V_{VR} represents the series and shunt source voltage magnitude, δ_{VR} and δ_{CR} represent the phase angle of series and shunt sources, G_{mn} and B_{mn} represents the conductance and susceptance between m^{th} and n^{th} bus, G_{VR} and B_{VR} are the susceptance and conductance between shunt and series voltage sources, V_m, and V_n are the voltages at m^{th} and n^{th} bus, θ_m and δ_n are the phase angles of mth and n^{th} bus, respectively.

5.3 Problem Formulation

In this research, multi-objective optimal DG and FACTS placement for EV load management deals with maximizing the annual profit while reducing power losses and raising of bus voltages to increase system efficiency and reliability. The total operating cost of a system is largely influenced by network losses and the cost of additional DG and FACTS devices integrated with it. Therefore, the total cost of losses in a system annually constitutes the cost of the extra load resulting from DG and FACTS integration as well as power distribution losses, whereas the operating cost without additional sources reflects energy losses only because of the power distribution cost.

TEL (US$) for the year without DG and FACTS devices can be calculated as:

$$\text{TEL}\left(\text{Without DG}\ \& FACTS\right) = \text{Energy}_{\text{Cost}} \tag{5.5}$$

where $Energy_{Cost} = Losses_{without\ DG\ \&\ FACTS} \times 0.05 \times 8760 \times 1000$ US$

US$ 0.06 is the cost of energy losses per Mw, 1000 US$ is the installation cost of shunt capacitors.

TEL (US$) for the year with DG and FACTS device integration can be calculated as:

$$\text{TEL}\left(\text{With DG}\ \& FACTS\right) = \text{Energy}_{\text{Cost}} + \text{DG}_{\text{Cost}} + \text{FACTS}_{\text{Cost}} \tag{5.6}$$

where $Energy_{Cost} = Losses_{with\ DG\ \&\ FACTS} \times 0.05 \times 8760 \times 1000$ US$

Total savings can be calculated as:

$$Savings = \left\{Total_{Cost}\left(without\ DG\ \& FACTS\right) - \left(with\ DG\ \& FACTS\right)\right\} \tag{5.7}$$

The current chapter focuses on developing a multi-objective function that reduces fuel costs for generation and power losses and optimizes the smaller size of DGs and UPFC installation costs to reduce total annual economic losses.

The multi-objective function formulated using more than one objective function can be described as follows:

$$F_{MO} = Min\left\{F_1(x), F_2(x), F_3(x), F(x)........F_n(x)\right\} \tag{5.8}$$

subject to $h(x) = 0$, and $g(x) \leq 0$,

where F_{MO} is the multi-objective function, $f_n(x)$ is the nth objective function of variable v, $h(x)$ is an equality constraint and $g(x)$ is an inequality constraint. In this study, four objectives were considered, therefore, n varied from 1 to 4.

The challenge in the multi-objective optimization problem is to choose the minimum value for each objective functions taken into consideration at a time for a particular solution. Therefore, the technique of multi-objective optimization is based on the Pareto dominance principle in which the optimal value is found based on the best compromise solution of all the objectives. A collection of non-dominated solutions, known as the Pareto optimal set (curve) or simply the Pareto set, provides the optimal solution when no objective can be improved without compromising at least one other objective.

5.4 Objective Functions

5.4.1 Reduction of power losses

The following equation provides the minimization function for power losses in the system

$$F_1(P_{Loss}) = \sum_{\substack{k=1 \\ l\neq 1}}^{n} C_{kl}\left(V_k^2 + V_l^2 - 2V_kV_l\cos(\delta_k - \delta_l)\right) \tag{5.9}$$

where n is the number of the transmission lines, C_{kl} represents the conductance between bus k and l, δ_k, and δ_l are the phase angles, V_k and V_l are the voltages of buses k and l, respectively.

5.4.2 Fuel cost reduction of thermal generators

The objective function for fuel cost is given as:

$$F_2(G_C) = u_ip_i^2 + v_ip_i + w_i \tag{5.10}$$

where P_i is the actual power generated by i_{th} generator and u_i, v_i, w_i represents the cost coefficients of i_{th} generator.

5.4.3 Cost reduction of DG units

The objective here is to optimize the smaller size of the DGs (P_{DG}) so that the total operating cost can be reduced. The objective function is formulated as follows:

$$F_3(DG_C) = \frac{C_{DG}\sum_{n=1}^{N} P_{DGn}}{L_{DG}} \tag{5.11}$$

where n is the number of DGs integrated into the system, C_{DG} is the price of power injected by DGs which includes capital investment as well as maintenance cost, L_{DG} is the life of DG which is usually 10 years.

5.4.4 Cost of UPFC device

It is important to calculate the investment cost of the UPFC controller, for which purpose the cost function is taken as

$$F_4\ (UPFC) = 0.0003s^2 - 0.026911s + 188.22 \tag{5.12}$$

$s = |Q_2| - |Q_1|$ is the working range of FACTS device

where Q_2 and Q_1 indicates flow of reactive power in line where UPFC is installed.

5.4.5 Equality and inequality constraints

System constraints must be satisfied in order to find the optimal solution. The various constraints areas:

$$\left.\begin{aligned} & V_{G_i}^{min} \le V_{G_i} \le V_{G_i}^{max}; \\ & P_{G_i}^{min} \le P_{G_i} \le P_{G_i}^{max}; \quad i = 1, 2, 3, \ldots\ldots n_G \\ & Q_{G_i}^{min} \le Q_{G_i} \le Q_{G_i}^{m}; \end{aligned}\right\} \tag{5.13}$$

where V_{G_i} is the voltage magnitude, P_{G_i} is the active power generation, and Q_{G_i} is the reactive power generation by i^{th} generator.

$$T_i^{min} \le T_i \le T_i^{max} \ ; \qquad i = 1, 2, 3\ldots\ldots n_T \tag{5.14}$$

where T_i is the transformer tab setting

$$Q_{Shi}^{\ min} \le Q_{Shi} \le Q_{Shi}^{\ \max} \ ; i = 1, 2, 3\ldots\ldots n_{Sh} \tag{5.15}$$

where Q_{Shi} is the shunt compensators at i^{th} bus

$$S_k \le S_k^{max} \ ; \qquad i = 1, 2, 3\ldots\ldots n_k \tag{5.16}$$

where S_k is the transmission line capacity for line k

$$P_m = |V_m| \sum_{n=1}^{k} \left(|V_n||Y_{mn}|\cos\left(\phi_{mn} + \delta_n - \delta_m\right)\right) \tag{5.17}$$

$$Q_m = -|V_m| \sum_{n=1}^{k} \left(|V_n||Y_{mn}|\sin\left(\phi_{mn} + \delta_n - \delta_m\right)\right) \tag{5.18}$$

where P_m, Q_m are the active and reactive power flow at m^{th} bus

$$P_{DG}^{\ min} \leq P_{DG} \leq P_{DG}^{\ max} \tag{5.19}$$

where P_{DG} is the power generated from DG energy sources

$$\left.\begin{array}{l} X_F^{min} \leq X_F \leq X_F^{max}; \\ V_{CR}^{min} \leq V_{CR} \leq V_{CR}^{max}; \\ V_{VR}^{min} \leq V_{VR} \leq V_{VR}^{max}; \\ \delta_{CR}^{min} \leq \delta_{CR} \leq \delta_{CR}^{max}; \\ \delta_{VR}^{min} \leq \delta_{VR} \leq \delta_{VR}^{m}; \end{array}\right\} \tag{5.20}$$

where X_F is the reactance of the FACTS device; V_{VR}, δ_{VR} and V_{CR}, δ_{CR} is the voltage and phase angle of the shunt and series sources, respectively.

5.4.5.1 EV SoC constraints

$$EV_{charging} \leq EV_{soc,min} \tag{5.21}$$

$$EV_{D,,min,soc} \leq EV_{discharge} \leq EV_{max,soc} \tag{5.22}$$

where $EV_{soc,min}$ is the minimum SoC level for charging, $EV_{max,soc}$ is the maximum permissible SoC level for discharging, $EV_{D,,min,soc}$ is the minimum SoC level for discharging.

The SoC of EVs monitoring is essential for G-2-V and V-2-G modes of operation. Here the value of $EV_{soc,min}$ is taken as 30%, it indicates EVs are connected in charging mode when SoC is less than 30%. The value of $EV_{D,,min,soc}$ and $EV_{max,soc}$ for V-2-G mode is taken as 40% and 90%, respectively. The EVs are not charged up to 100% to limit overcharging and health degradation.

5.4.5.2 EV power balance constraints

$$P_{bc,L} + P_{EV,charging}(t) + P_{loss}(t) = P_L(t) \tag{5.23}$$

$$P_L(t) = P_G(t) + P_{EV,discharging}(\text{t}) \tag{5.24}$$

Here $P_{bc,L}$ is the base case load, $P_{EV,charging}$ is the EVs charging load connected to network, $P_{EV,charging}$ is the power required during charging of EVs at any instant t, P_{loss} is the active losses at any instant t, P_L is the total load at any instant t, P_G

is the power produced by generators present, $P_{EV,discharging}$ is the power generated by EVs during the discharging process at any instant t.

5.4.5.3 Power requirement for EV charging

$$P^{EV} = P^{EV}_{EV,rated} \star \left(\sum_{i=1}^{N_{bus}} \sum_{k \in \Omega_t^{EV}} B_{k,j} \right) \qquad \forall_{SRDN}, \forall_i \in \Omega_{CF} \tag{5.25}$$

This constraint shows the availability of power after satisfying the consumer base load.

5.4.5.4 Availability of EV charging/discharging facilities

$$N_J^{CF} \geq \sum_{i=1}^{N_{bus}} \sum_{k \in \Omega_t^{EV}} B_{k,j} \qquad \forall, \forall_i \in \Omega_{CF} \tag{5.26}$$

N_j^{CF} is the number of charging/discharging facilities installed at bus j, Ω_{CF} number of buses where car parking stations (CPS) are installed. The installed CPS must satisfy the charging facility for N number of vehicles at any season at any time.

5.5 Results and Discussion

The proposed strategy is deployed on a Desktop-3M7ESSE employing an Intel(R) Core (TM) 2DuoCPU T6570 @ 2.10 GHz with setup memory of 6.00 GB and a 64-bit operating system. To perform the load flow studies, an IEEE-30 bus system was taken, and codes were run on MATLAB 2020a software. The IEEE-30 bus system includes 24 load buses, 41 branch lines, and six generators on bus locations 1, 2, 5, 8, 11 and 13. Table 5.1 shows the generator power limits and cost coefficient values. Tables 5.2 and 5.3 present the parameter setting and control variables used in MO techniques for ODGFP. Bus 1 is considered as Slack bus. The total generation capacity of the IEEE-30 bus system is 900.2 MW, with a range of -102 MVar to 188 MVar. The economic benefits of ODGFP for a utility can be explained by the annual reduction in energy losses reduced for a system annually. Only a portion of its lifespan is used to improve power losses and voltage instability. The capital investment for DG units which involves installation, maintenance, and operation is included in the cost of power injected by DGs taken to be US$ 20.00/Mw. To demonstrate the optimization potential of the proposed methods, the results of interest are marked in bold in Tables 5.5-5.6, and ranking is also provided based on savings obtained from the following cases studied under different scenarios.

Four cases were studied under this scenario:

- Case 1: EV load management with 1DG and UPFC controller
- Case 2: EV load management with 2DGs and UPFC controller
- Case 3: EV load management with 3DGs and UPFC controller
- Case 4: EV load management with 4DGs and UPFC controller

Table 5.1 Cost coefficients and generator limits of IEEE-30 for DG-UPFC installation.

Bus no.	a (US$/MW2h)	b (US$/MWh)	c (US$/h)	P_{min} (MW)	P_{max} (MW)
1	0.00375	2	0	50	200
2	0.01750	1.75	0	20	80
5	0.062	1	0	15	50
8	0.008	3.25	0	10	55
11	0.025	3	0	10	30
13	0.025	3	0	12	40

Table 5.2 Parameter setting values for DG-UPFC installation.

Algorithm	Parameter	Value
MODE	Population size	50
	No. of iterations	100
	Crossover's Constant (C_r)	0.9
	Scaling Factor (F)	0.7
	Independent Runs	30
MOGWO	Number of wolves	50
	No. of iterations	100
	Coefficient Vector ($\vec{x}$)	[0,2]
	Random Vectors ($\vec{u_1}$, $\vec{u_2}$)	[0,1]
	Independent Runs	30

Table 5.3 Control variables settings for DG-UPFC installation.

Variable	Range
DG_{Size}	[10, 300]
X_F	[-0.2, 0.8]
V_{VR}	[0.9, 1.05]
V_{CR}	[0.9, 1.05]
δ_{VR}	[0, π]
δ_{CR}	[0, π]

Variable	Range
Generator Voltages	[0.98,1.08]
Transformer Taps	[0.9, 1]
Shunt Capacitors (Q_{SH})	[0, 0.15]
Reactive Generation (MVar)	[-50, 100]

5.5.1 EV load management using DG and UPFC controller

In a standard loading scenario, the IEEE-30 bus system carries a total load of 283.4 MW and 126.2 MVar. According to the N-R load flow analysis, there are real power losses of 17.55 MW and reactive power losses of 67.69 MVar, based on a 100 MVA base case. Under these conditions, the total power generation is 300.9 MW, with Generator 1 supplying 260.96 MW and Generator 2 providing 40 MW. When the load is increased due to the addition of EVCS at load buses 10, 12, 14, 16, and 17 chosen for their minimal voltage variation an extra 7.2 KW load taken from [172] is also added to each bus, enabling consumers to charge their vehicles at home. As a result, the total load increases to 301.59 MW, power losses grow to 19.97 MW, and power generation rises to 321.52 MW, with the fuel cost reaching US$ 958.24 per hour for the base case. TEL for the base case amount to 7.687× US$. After optimizing the system by adding a DG-UPFC controller into the system, Figure 5.2 shows the improvement in each branch line. The non-dominated solutions for different cases in this EV loading scenario are shown in Figure 5.3. Further, the comparative results of the total power loss improvement for both the models are shown in Figure 5.4.

Figure 5.2 Line losses improvement for IEEE-30 with DG-UPFC controller.

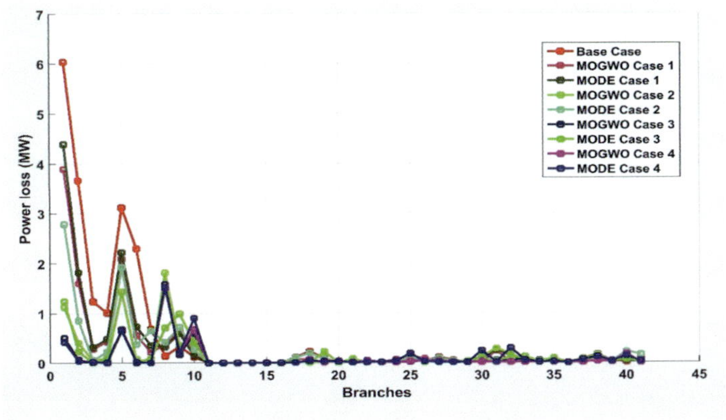

Figure 5.3 Non dominated solutions for EV loading: (a, b, c) 1DG-UPFC; (d, e, f) 2DG-UPFC; (g, h, i) 3DG-UPFC; (j, k, l) 4DG-UPFC.

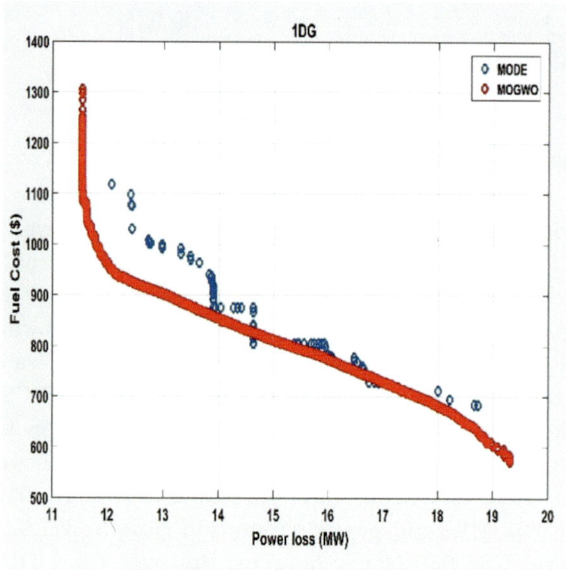

(a)

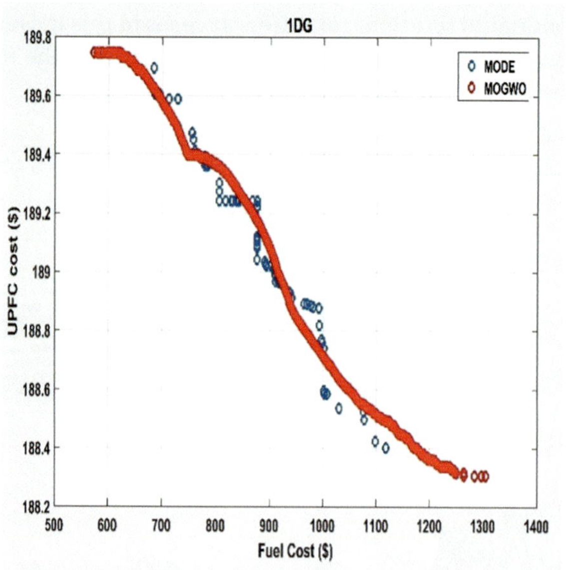

(b)

Figure 5.3 *Continued*

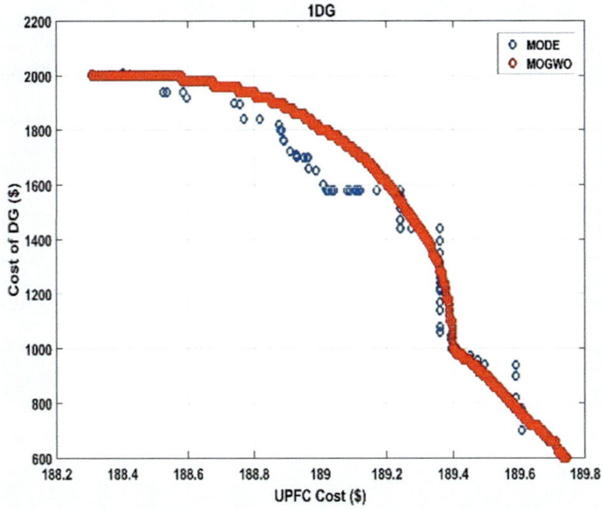

(c)

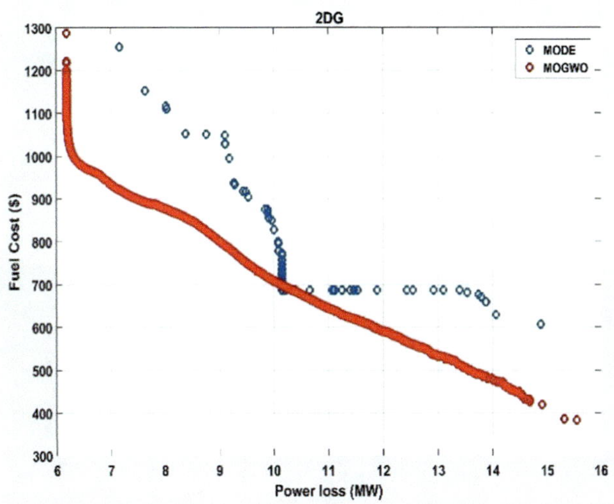

(d)

(*Continued*)

Figure 5.3 *Continued*

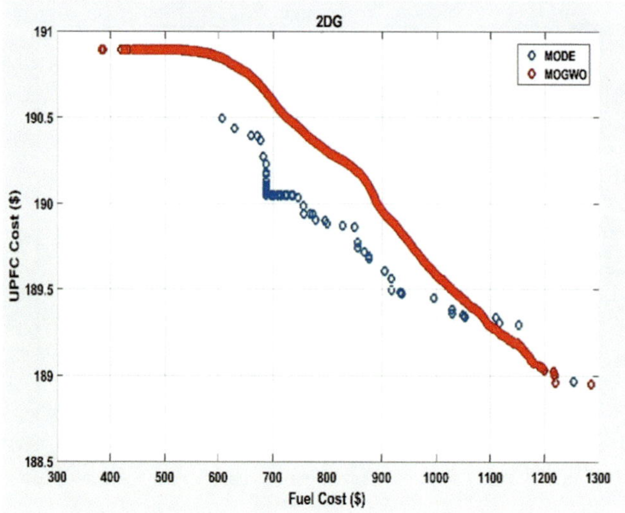

(e)

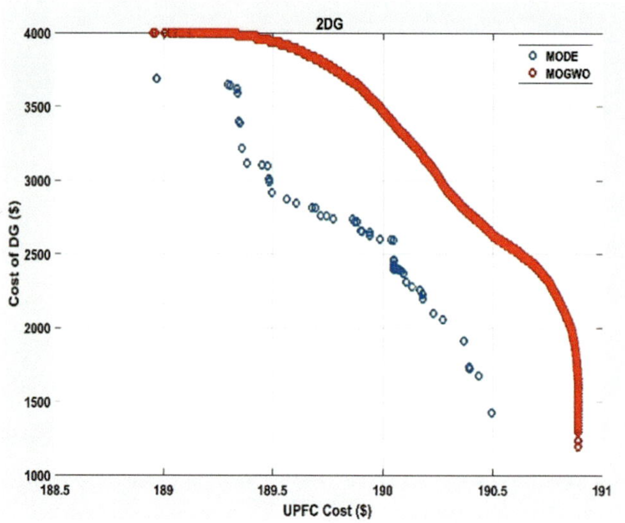

(f)

Figure 5.3 *Continued*

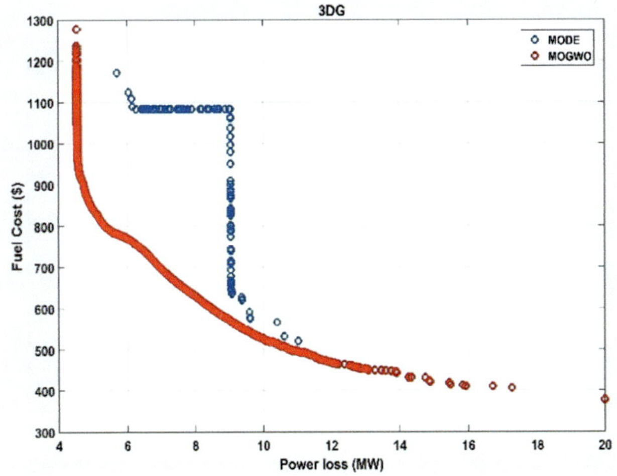

(g)

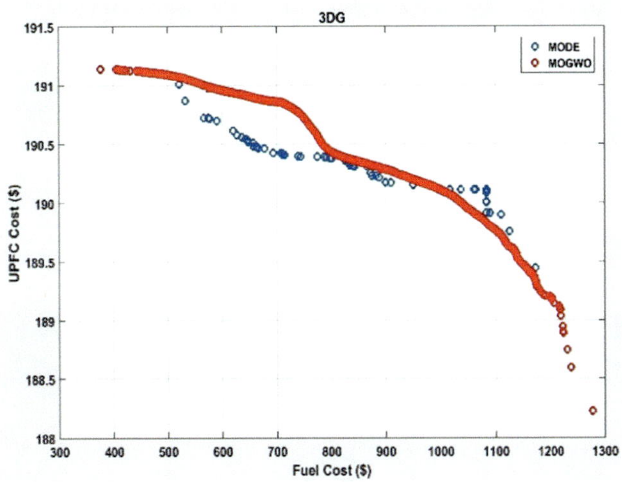

(h)

(Continued)

Figure 5.3 *Continued*

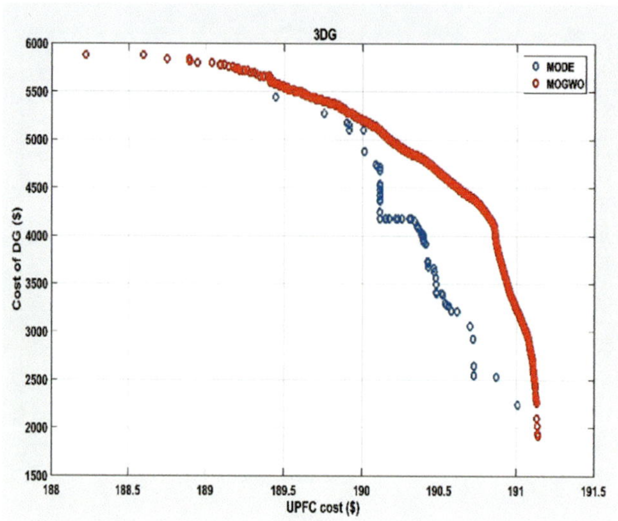

(i)

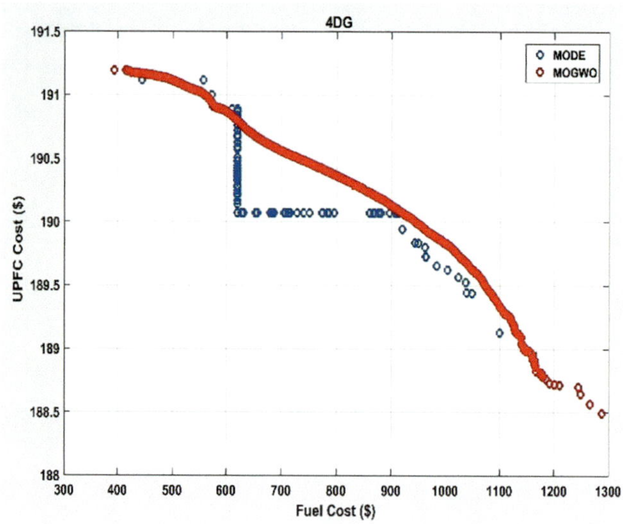

(j)

Figure 5.3 *Continued*

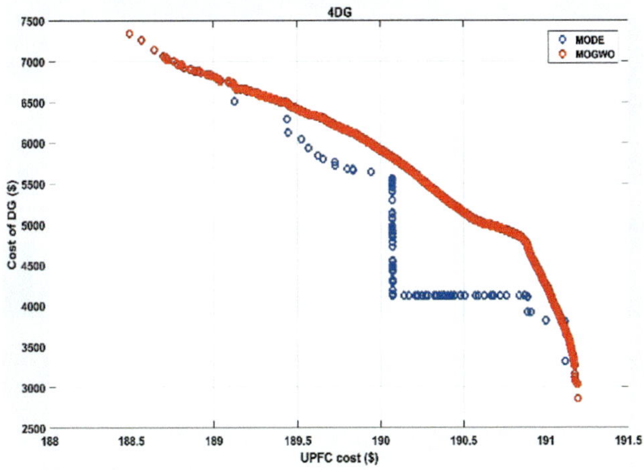

(k)

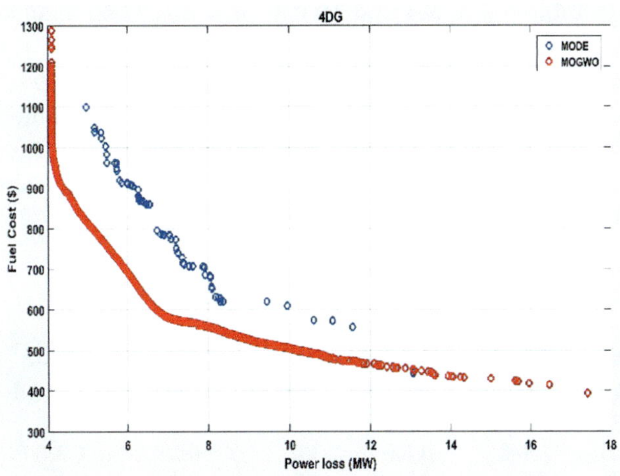

(l)

Figure 5.4 Total power losses improvement in IEEE-30 bus system with DG-UPFC.

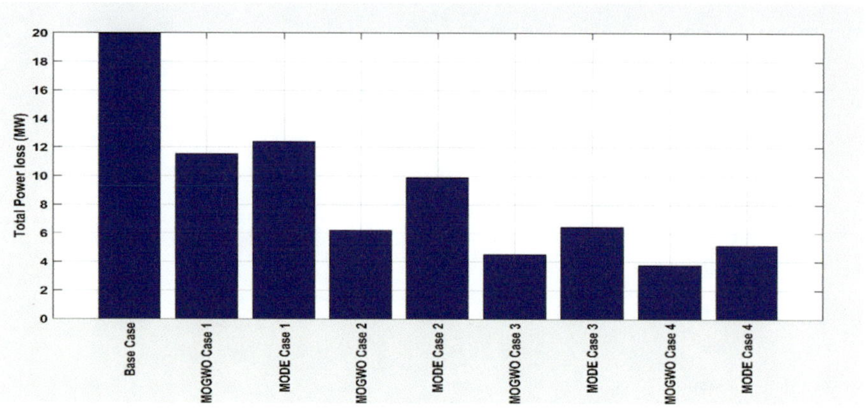

Table 5.3 provides the percentage of savings obtained with the addition of DGs units with UPFC into the system to reduce annual economic losses. Table 5.4 shows the reactive power loss (MVar) improvement with and without DGs and UPFC. Table 5.5 shows that MODE provides 37.90%, 50.47%, 67.80% and 74.11% of decrease in power losses for cases 1, 2, 3 and 4, respectively from base case where as MOGWO approach provides 42.26%, 69% 77.31% and 80.12% for cases 1, 2, 3 and 4, respectively from base case and Table 5.6 provides the comparison of TEL for EV loading in IEEE-30 bus system. Therefore, from the results, case 4 with MOGWO is considered as the optimum solution for DG and UPFC placement.

Table 5.4 Reactive power losses in lines with and without DG-UPFC controller for EV loading.

Line no.	Base Case	MODE (case 4)	MOGWO (case 4)	Line no.	Base Case	MODE (case 4)	MOGWO (case 4)
1	18.074	1.277	1.087	**19**	0.184	0.062	0.015
2	13.405	0.146	0.148	**20**	0.001	0.010	0.052
3	3.775	0.050	0.066	**21**	0.013	0.001	0.015
5	13.09	2.875	2.860	**24**	0.037	0.005	0.006
6	6.962	0.063	0.061	**25**	0.195	0.019	0.045
7	2.411	0.003	0.007	**26**	0.097	0.053	0.097
8	0.356	0.167	0.145	**27**	0.234	0.010	0.045
9	1.037	0.529	0.547	**28**	0.105	0.001	0.019
10	0.417	1.173	1.088	**29**	0.001	0.007	0.006
17	0.241	0.003	0.001	**31**	0.063	0.018	0.008
18	0.451	0.060	0.085	**37**	0.163	0.109	0.009

The convergence characteristics of the objective functions are shown in Figure 5.5. This plot effectively demonstrates that the MOGWO algorithm outperforms the MODE algorithm across all tested cases in terms of reaching lower objective values and achieving better convergence. This suggests that MOGWO may be more suitable for complex multi-objective optimization problems like power system planning, DG and FACTS placement, or EV load scheduling, depending on the application.

Table 5.5 Result summary of optimal power flow output with DG-UPFC controller under both models.

Case	Method	DGs Optimal Sitting/Size (MW)	UPFC Sitting/ Size (MVar)	Power Losses (MW)	Fuel Cost (US$/h)	DGs Cost (US$)	UPFC Cost (US$)
1	MODE	24/92	12/26.76	12.40	829.67	1840	189.60
	MOGWO	9/100	10/44.62	11.53	935.76	2000	189.39
2	MODE	4/81; 28/57	1/0.31	9.89	715.29	2760	189.48
	MOGWO	7/100;24/100	22/5.85	6.19	886.85	4000	190.89
3	MODE	9/99; 16/61; 23/41	14/4.68	6.43	774.98	4020	190.37
	MOGWO	7/68;9/100; 15/74	1/12.88	4.53	784.00	4840	190.85
4	MODE	7/56; 6/70; 20/53;23/75	23/7.39	5.17	859.88	5080	191.11
	MOGWO	7/58; 9/100; 15/62; 30/30	6/17.8	**3.97**	**572.00**	**5000**	**190.89**

Table 5.6 Comparison of TEL in IEEE-30 bus test system for EV loading.

TEL_{Base} (US$) [A]	Case	Method	$TEL_{DG\ \&\ UPFC}$ (US$) [B]	Savings (US$) [A-B]	Savings (%)
7.687×10^6	1	MODE	5.43×10^6	2.257×10^6	29.3
		MOGWO	5.05×10^6	2.637×10^6	34.3
	2	MODE	4.33×10^6	3.357×10^6	43.6
		MOGWO	2.71×10^6	4.977×10^6	64.7
	3	MODE	2.81×10^6	4.877×10^6	63.4
		MOGWO	1.98×10^6	5.707×10^6	74.2
	4	MODE	2.26×10^6	5.427×10^6	70.5
		MOGWO	$\mathbf{1.73 \times 10^6}$	$\mathbf{5.957 \times 10^6}$	**77.4**

Figure 5.5 Convergence characteristics of MODE and MOGWO for multi-DG and UPFC controller.

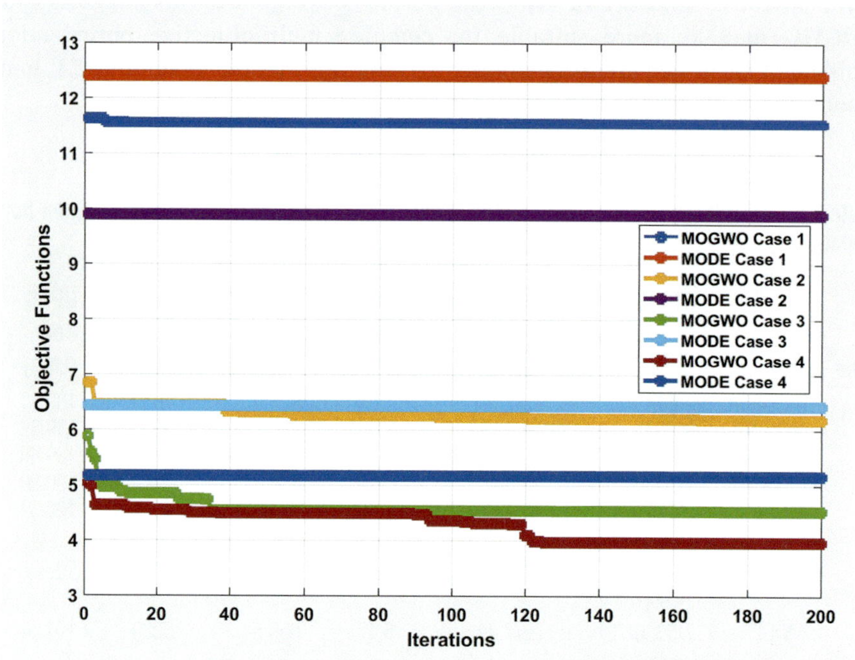

5.5.2 Impact on bus voltage stability

The voltage profiles across 30 buses with different cases for both before and after optimization using the MODE and MOGWO models are shown in Figure 5.6. The voltage for base case is shown by the red line that depicts notable voltage decrease below 1 pu at bus 26 and below 0.94 pu at bus 30. The optimization findings for the employment of different DG integrations with the UPFC controller demonstrate considerable gains in voltage magnitude as compared to findings obtained with DG only (discussed in Chapter 4). MOGWO technique with case 4 maintains the most consistent and high voltage profile close to 1.08 pu that indicates its effectiveness in providing most stable voltage levels across the system. All bus voltage magnitudes were raised, with minimum and maximum limits of 0.99 pu and 1.08 pu being maintained throughout all evaluations. The simulation findings show that with an increasing number of

DG units and UPFC, a steady-state voltage profile can be observed after bus 9 and the weakest buses are 5 and 8 for all cases.

Figure 5.6 Bus voltage improvement with DG-UPFC integration.

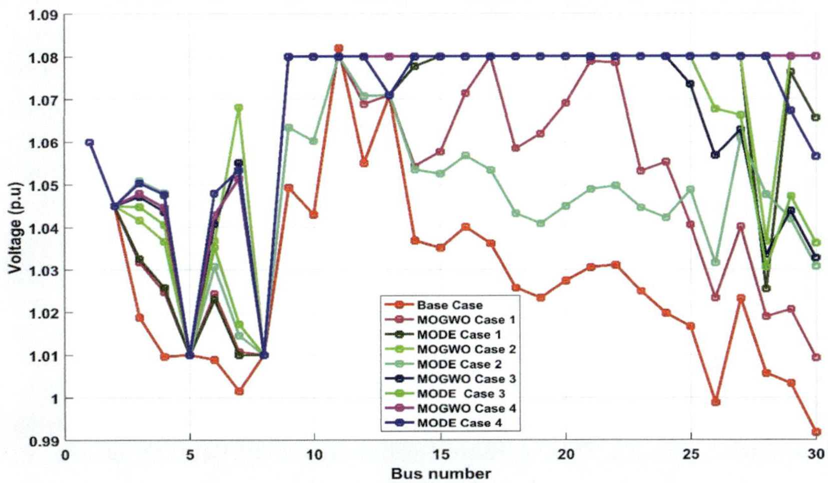

5.6 Conclusion

The optimal placement and sizing of DG and UPFC controllers within power distribution systems have emerged as critical strategies for enhancing overall network performance. This integrated approach can lead to substantial improvements in several key areas of power system operations. First, it significantly enhances the voltage profile across the network, ensuring that voltage levels remain within acceptable limits even during periods of high demand or fluctuating renewable energy generation. Second, it contributes to a marked reduction in power losses, which translates to improved energy efficiency and reduced operational costs for utilities.

Therefore, for EV load management using DG and UPFC, it was found that TEL reduced by 77.4%, generation cost was 40.3%, minimum value for power loss was 3.97 MW, and fuel cost was 572 US$/h. The results demonstrate a significant enhancement in power grid performance through the simultaneous conglomeration of DG-UPFC controllers. Despite the intermittent nature of

DGs, a stable voltage profile of 1.08 pu magnitude is maintained across most of buses with 4DGs.

This stability is achieved through the ability of the UPFC controller to effectively regulate voltage levels by dynamically absorbing or injecting reactive power as needed. The UPFC compensates for the voltage fluctuations caused by DG intermittency, ensuring consistent power quality throughout the grid. Therefore, the proposed approach significantly reduces the TEL and fuel costs of thermal power plants, which in turn helps power utilities minimize the total operating costs of the system. The computational time under all scenarios for MODE was 183.11 seconds and 120.05 seconds for MOGWO. Thus, it can be concluded that the proposed approach is a useful technique for acquiring affordable solutions for large-scale power systems. For future studies, it is recommended that other fault scenarios with different types of energy sources and multiple FACTS be investigated to improve the reliability of the system. In addition, the incorporation of machine learning with these optimization models opens future opportunities.

Moreover, the strategic deployment of DG and UPFC units bolsters overall system stability, making the network more resilient to disturbances and potential outages. This increased reliability is particularly crucial in an era of growing electricity demand and increasing integration of intermittent renewable energy sources. The approach not only enhances the reliability of the distribution network but also plays a pivotal role in facilitating the efficient utilization of renewable energy sources, which are becoming increasingly prevalent in modern power systems. The multi-objective optimization framework employed in this approach allows for a balanced consideration of various technical and economic factors. This comprehensive methodology considers diverse objectives such as minimizing power losses, improving voltage profiles, reducing operational costs, and maximizing the integration of renewable energy sources. By simultaneously optimizing these multiple objectives, the framework ensures a more holistic and sustainable solution for modern power distribution systems.

Furthermore, this approach addresses the complex interplay between different system components and operational constraints. It considers factors such as network topology, load variability, generation characteristics, and regulatory requirements. This holistic view enables system planners and operators to make informed decisions that balance short-term operational efficiency with long-term sustainability goals. The implementation of such optimized DG and FACT placement strategies also contributes to the concept of smart grids, enhancing grid flexibility and adaptability. This increased flexibility is crucial for managing the challenges posed by the growing penetration of EVs, energy storage systems, and presume-based energy trading models. Ultimately, this integrated and optimized approach to DG and FACTS placement and sizing represents a significant step towards creating more efficient, reliable, and sustainable power distribution systems for the future.

CHAPTER

6

Smart Grid Futures: Challenges, Trends, and Opportunities

6.1 Introduction

The global power sector is undergoing a historic transformation, driven by the dual imperatives of decarbonization and digitalization. Smart grids, as the next-generation evolution of conventional power systems, are central to this transition—serving as adaptive, data-rich, and resilient infrastructures capable of integrating a diverse array of energy resources while meeting increasingly complex consumer demands. Unlike the traditional unidirectional power flow paradigm, smart grids embody a dynamic, bidirectional, and highly interactive network in which generation, transmission, distribution, storage, and consumption are intelligently coordinated.

Throughout this book, it has been examined how EVs, DG, and FACTS form the technological triad that underpins smart grid flexibility and stability. EVs, with their rapidly increasing penetration, are no longer simply transportation assets but active participants in energy systems capable of influencing demand patterns, supporting ancillary services, and providing distributed storage. DG, particularly from renewable energy sources, decentralizes generation, reduces transmission losses, and enables localized energy resilience. FACTS devices, in turn, provide the critical control and compensation capabilities needed to manage the variability and intermittency introduced by both EV charging behaviour and renewable-based DG outputs.

As these technologies mature and proliferate, the smart grid is entering a new phase of complexity and opportunity. On the one hand, the network

DOI: 10.1201/9788743811176-6

must accommodate unprecedented levels of variability, both on the supply side due to the fluctuating nature of renewable DG and on the demand side, driven by stochastic EV charging loads and evolving consumer usage patterns. On the other hand, advancements in communication networks, IoT integration, artificial intelligence, and power electronics offer powerful tools to manage this complexity, enabling predictive control, real-time optimization, and market innovation. The coming decade will see the convergence of these technologies with multi-objective optimization algorithms, blockchain enabled energy transactions, hybrid storage systems, and next-generation FACTS controllers, potentially transforming the operational philosophy of power systems from reactive management to proactive orchestration. However, this vision is not without challenges ranging from cyber-physical vulnerabilities and regulatory inertia to integration complexity and economic feasibility.

Figure 6.1 looks ahead to the future of smart grids in the EV–DG–FACTS era, identifying the critical challenges that must be addressed, the emerging technological and operational trends shaping the sector, and the research and market opportunities that lie at the intersection of engineering innovation and energy policy. By situating these developments within the broader context of sustainable energy electricity network capable of supporting the global shift toward low-carbon, high reliability energy systems.

Figure 6.1 Smart grid futures roadmap (2030+ vision).

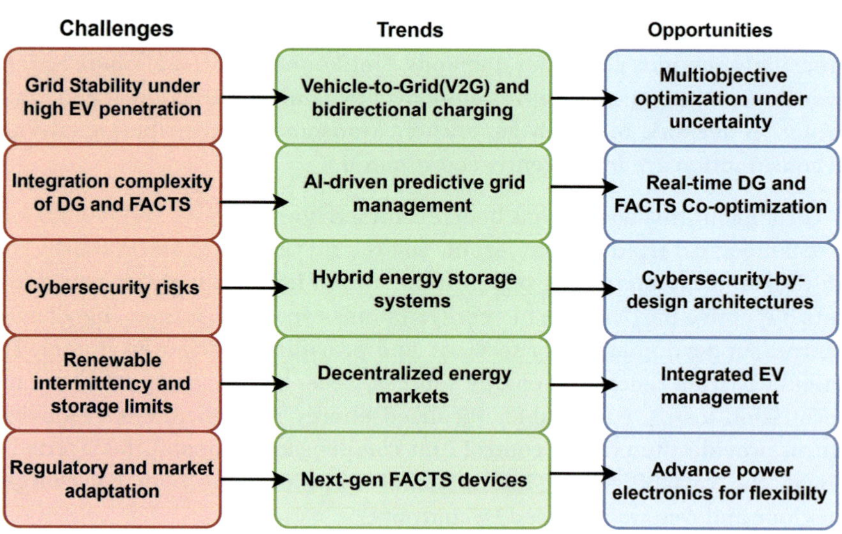

6.2 Key Challenges in the Next Decade

6.2.1 Grid stability under high EV penetration

The widespread adoption of EVs will introduce highly variable and stochastic charging loads. Without intelligent charging coordination and load balancing, peak demand could cause voltage fluctuations, overload distribution transformers, and accelerate asset degradation.

6.2.2 Integration complexity of DG and FACTS

While DG and FACTS individually enhance grid flexibility and reliability, coordinated integration presents complex technical challenges. FACTS control settings may conflict with DG operational strategies if not optimally tuned, potentially leading to suboptimal power flows or oscillations.

6.2.3 Cybersecurity risks

Smart grids rely heavily on IoT-enabled sensors, communication networks, and digital control systems, making them vulnerable to cyberattacks. Data breaches, malicious control overrides, or denial-of-service attacks could disrupt operations or compromise safety.

6.2.4 Renewable intermittency and storage limitations

DG resources, particularly solar and wind, face generation variability due to weather patterns. Without cost-effective, scalable energy storage solutions, ensuring consistent supply-demand balance remains a pressing challenge.

6.2.5 Regulatory and market adaptation

The pace of technological evolution often outstrips policy development. Regulatory frameworks must adapt to enable fair market participation for distributed assets, incentivize grid-supportive EV charging behaviour, and standardize FACTS deployment practices.

6.3 Emerging Trends Shaping the Future

6.3.1 Vehicle-to-Grid (V2G) and bidirectional charging

V2G technology enables EVs to function as mobile energy storage units, returning stored electricity to the grid during peak demand. This trend will transform EVs from passive consumers to active consumers, enhancing DR capabilities.

6.3.2 AI-driven predictive grid management

Machine learning algorithms and digital twins will allow utilities to predict demand surges, component failures, and renewable generation patterns with high accuracy, enabling primitive adjustments to DG output, FACTS settings, and EV charging schedules.

6.3.3 Hybrid Energy Storage Systems (HESS)

Combining battery storage with supercapacitors or flywheels will provide both short-term power buffering and long-term energy shifting, improving voltage stability and frequency regulation.

6.3.4 Decentralized energy markets

Blockchain enabled peer-to-peer energy trading will allow consumers to sell excess solar energy or stored EV battery power directly to others, bypassing traditional intermediaries while still ensuring grid reliability.

6.3.5 FACTS device evolution

Next-generation FACTS devices will feature modular, plug and play architectures with self-tuning capabilities. These will enable dynamic reconfiguration of transmission capacity and voltage profiles without extensive human intervention.

6.4 Opportunities for Research and Innovation

6.4.1 Multi-objective optimization under uncertainty

Future research should focus on metaheuristic algorithms capable of handling the uncertainties introduced by high renewable penetration, EV load variability, and dynamic FACTS control requirements.

6.4.2 Real-time DG and FACTS co-optimization platforms

Developing cloud-based platforms for real-time monitoring, simulation, and co-optimization will empower operators to dynamically adjust device parameters for optimal performance.

6.4.3 Cybersecurity by design architectures

Rather than retrofitting security measures, future smart grids should integrate cybersecurity at the design stage, using AI-based intrusion detection and self-healing network topologies.

6.4.4 Integrated EV fleet management for grid support

Coordinating large EV fleets for DR and frequency regulation can unlock significant ancillary service potential, reducing dependence on conventional peaking plants.

6.4.5 Advanced power electronics for grid flexibility

Innovations in wide bandgap semiconductor devices will enhance FACTS performance, enabling faster response times, higher efficiency, and greater adaptability to varying grid conditions.

6.5 Conclusion

The future of smart grids will be defined by synergy between advanced technologies where EVs act as flexible loads and storage assets, DG sources provide clean and DG, and FACTS devices ensure robust power flow control. However, realizing this vision demands coordinated technical, regulatory, and economic strategies, supported by cutting-edge optimization techniques, intelligent control systems, and secure communication networks. As the global energy landscape shifts toward decarbonization, resilience, and digitalization, the integration of EVs, DG, and FACTS will remain at the heart of the smart grid evolution. Those who can effectively harness these technologies while overcoming associated challenges will shape the next generation of sustainable and intelligent power systems.

References

[1] Xue Q (2022) Increasing commitment to the sustainable development goals across universities worldwide. Sustainable Horizons 2:100021–100032.

[2] Filote C, Felseghi R-A, Raboaca MS, Achilean I (2020) Environmental impact assessment of green energy systems for power supply of electric vehicle charging station. Int J Energy Res 44(13) 10471.

[3] Singh B, Jain V, Chandra SA, Al-Haddad K (2021) Power quality improvement in a PV based EV charging station interfaced with three phase grid. Toronto: IECON 2021 47th Annual Conference of the IEEE Industrial Electronics Society 1–6.

[4] Kumar U, Vadhera S (2023) Optimal allocation of electric vehicle charging station with distribution generation and D-STATCOM using grey wolf optimization. Advances in Renewable Energy and Its Grid Integration. ICAER Lecture Notes in Electrical Engineering, vol 1041. Springer, Singapore.

[5] Bilal M, Rizwan M, Alsaidan I, Almasoudi FM (2021) AI-based approach for optimal placement of EVCS and DG with reliability analysis. IEEE Access 9:154204–154224.

[6] Lone RA, Javed Iqbal S, Anees AS (2023) Optimal location and sizing of distributed generation for distribution systems: An improved analytical technique. International Journal of Green Energy 21(3) 682–700.

[7] Kumar A, Verma R, Choudhary NK, Singh N (2023) Optimal placement and sizing of distributed generation in power distribution system: a comprehensive review. Energy Sources Part A: Recovery, Utilization, and Environmental Effects 45(3) 7160–7185.

[8] Ewaoche OJ, Nwulu N (2018) Design and simulation of UPFC and IPFC for voltage stability under a single line contingency: A comparative study. In Proceedings of the International Conference on Industrial Engineering and Operations Management, Washington DC, USA, 27-29 September 2018; IEOM Society International: Washington DC, USA.

[9] Ewaoche OJ, Nwulu N (2018) Modelling and simulation of interline power flow controller for improved transmission system security. In Proceedings of the International Conference on Computational Techniques, Electronics and Mechanical Systems (CTEMS), Belgaum, India, 21–22 December 2018; IEEE: Belgaum, India, pp. 250–255.

[10] Ewaoche OJ, Nwulu N (2018) Fault clearance and transmission system stability enhancement using unified power flow controller. In Proceedings of the International Conference on Computational Techniques, Electronics and Mechanical Systems (CTEMS), Belgaum, India, 21–22 December 2018; IEEE: Belgaum, India, pp. 86–91.

[11] Wong M-C, Lam C-S, Wang L, Choi W-H (2019) Smarter Solutions Based on Power Electronics. Amsterdam: Elsevier.

[12] Ahmad AL, Sirjani R (2019) Optimal placement and sizing of multi-type FACTS devices in power systems using metaheuristic optimisation techniques: An updated review. Ain Shams Eng J 11:611–628.

[13] Chethan M, Kuppan R (2024) A review of FACTS device implementation in power systems using optimization techniques. J Eng Appl Sci 71:18.

[14] Hagh MT, Borhany MAJ, Taghizad-Tavana K, Oskouei MZ (2025) A comprehensive review of flexible alternating current transmission system (FACTS): Topologies, applications, optimal placement, and innovative models. Heliyon 11(1).

[15] EV boosters powering charging careers https://evboosters.com/ev-charging-news/global-ev-outlook-2024-ev-sales-set-to-reach-17-million/

[16] Zhou X, Zou L, Ma Y, Gao Z (2017) Research on impacts of the electric vehicles charging and discharging on power grid. In 2017 29th Chinese Control and Decision Conference (CCDC) 1398–1402.

[17] Di Lorenzo G, Yadiyal K (2024) Sustainable power system planning for India: Insights from a modelling and simulation perspective. Energy Nexus 13: 100261.

[18] Hingorani NG (1998) High power electronics and flexible AC transmission system. IEEE Power Review 8(7) 3–4.

[19] Gadal R et al. (2023) Voltage stability assessment and control using indices and FACTS: A comparative review. Journal of Electrical and Computer Engineering (1) 1–18.

[20] Sharma S et al (2024) A comprehensive review on STATCOM: Paradigm of modeling, control, stability, optimal location, integration, application and installation. IEEE Access 12: 2701–2729.

[21] Ranjan S, Das DC, Sinha N, Latif A, Hussain SMS, Ustun TS (2021) Voltage stability assessment of isolated hybrid dish-Stirling solar thermal-diesel microgrid with STATCOM using mine blast algorithm. Electric Power Systems Research 196(July) 107239.

[22] Singh RK, Singh NK (2022) Power system transient stability improvement with FACTS controllers using SSSC-based controller. Sustainable Energy Technologies and Assessments 53:102664.

[23] Georgilakis PS, Hatziargyriou ND (2019) Unified power flow controllers in smart power systems: Models, methods and future research. IET Smart Grid 2(1) 2–10.

[24] Marouani I et al (2023) Optimized FACTS devices for power system enhancement: Applications and solving methods. Sustainability 15(12) 9348.

[25] Chakraborty S, Verma S, Salgotra A, Elavarasan RM, Elangovan D, Mihet-Popa L (2021) Solar-based DG allocation using Harris Hawk's optimization while considering practical aspects. Energies 14:1–26.

[26] Sunil A, Venkaiah C (2023) Optimal power dispatch of multiple DGs using a hybrid algorithm for mitigating voltage deviations and losses in a radial distribution system with economic benefits. Distributed Generation and Alternative Energy Journal 38:1531–1558.

[27] Shehata AA, Tolba MA, El-Rifaie AA, Korovkin NV (2022) Power system operation enhancement using a new hybrid methodology for optimal allocation of FACTS devices. Energy Reports 8:217–238.

[28] Rao NT, Sankar MM, Rao SP, Rao BS (2021) Comparative study of Pareto optimal multi-objective cuckoo search algorithm and multi-objective particle swarm optimization for power loss minimization incorporating UPFC. Journal of Ambient Intelligence and Humanized Computing 12:1069–1080.

[29] Reddy HK, Reddy PRK, Ganesh V (2019) Optimal allocation of multiple FACTS devices with hybrid techniques for improving voltage stability. International Journal of Emerging Technology 10:76–84.

[30] Nadeem M, Imran K, Khattak A, Ulasyar A, Pal A, Zeb MZ, Khan AN, Padhee M (2020) Optimal placement, sizing and coordination of FACTS devices in transmission network using whale optimization algorithm. Energies 13:753.

[31] Muhammad Y, Khan R, Raja MAZ, Ullah F, Chaudhary NI, He Y (2020) Design of fractional swarm intelligent computing with entropy evolution for optimal power flow problems. IEEE Access 8:111401–111419.

[32] Rafee SM, Reddy AS (2021) Enhancing system loadability with multiple FACTS devices using artificial bee colony algorithm. Advances in Smart Grid Technology 700:311–322.

[33] Amarendra A, Srinivas LR, Srinivasa Rao R (2022) Power system security enhancement in FACTS devices based on yin–yang pair optimization algorithm. Soft Computing 26:6265–6291.

[34] Khan NH et al (2021) A novel modified lightning attachment procedure optimization technique for optimal allocation of the FACTS devices in power systems. IEEE Access 9:47976–47997.

[35] Amarendra A, Srinivas LR, Rao RS (2021) Security enhancement in power system using FACTS devices and atom search optimization algorithm. EAI Endorsed Transactions on Energy Web 8(36) e9.

[36] Eladl AA, Basha MI, El Desouky AA (2022) Multi-objective based reactive power planning and voltage stability enhancement using FACTS and capacitor banks. Electrical Engineering 106:3173–3196.

[37] Mohamed S, Anwer AN, Mahmoud MM (2023) Solving optimal power flow problem for IEEE-30 bus system using a developed particle swarm optimization method: Towards fuel cost minimization. International Journal of Modelling and Simulation 1–14.

[38] Panthagani P, Rao RS (2020) Pareto-based allocations of multitype flexible AC transmission system devices for optimal reactive power dispatch using kinetic gas molecule optimization algorithm. Measurement and Control 53:239–249.

[39] Shaheen MAM, Hasanien HM, Alkuhayli A (2021) A novel hybrid GWO-PSO optimization technique for optimal reactive power dispatch problem solution. Ain Shams Engineering Journal 12:621–630.

[40] Daealhaq HM, Kfajey YF, Tukkee AS (2021) Power loss reduction and voltage profile improvement using optimal placement of FACTS devices. In IOP Conference Series: Materials Science and Engineering 1067:012128.

[41] Reddy G et al (2022) Optimal sizing and allocation of DG and FACTS device in the distribution system using fractional Lévy flight bat algorithm. IFAC-Papers On Line 55(1) 168–173.

[42] Biswas P et al (2021) Optimal placement and sizing of FACTS devices for optimal power flow in a wind power integrated electrical network. Neural Computing and Applications 33:6753–6774.

[43] Iweh C D, Gyamfi S, Tanyi E, Effah-Donyina E (2021) Distributed generation and renewable energy integration into the grid: prerequisites, push factors, practical options, issues and merits. Energies 14(17) 5375.

[44] Allan G, Eromenko I, Gilmartin M, Kockar I, McGregor P (2015) The economics of distributed energy generation: A literature review. Renew Sustain Energy Rev 543–556.

[45] Dommel HW, Tinney WF (1968) Optimal power flow solutions. IEEE Transactions on Power Apparatus and Systems PAS-87(10) 1866–1876.

[46] Saddique MA, Bhatti A, Marwat AK, Ali A (2025) Reactive power optimization in smart grids with intermittent renewable sources. Energy Reports 13:397–423.

[47] Soto R, Gámez JA, Molina JM (2001) Reactive power optimization using meta-heuristics: A comparative study. Applied Soft Computing 1(2) 127–138.

[48] Suresh V, Senthil Kumar C (2025) ORPD using evolutionary computation in renewable-integrated systems. Energy Reports 13:397–423.

[49] Khan MH, Abo-Hammour ZA, Saleh SA (2022) Voltage stability enhancement using metaheuristic optimization. IEEE Access 10:7564–7576.

[50] Bhattacharyya B, Karmakar N (2020) Optimal reactive power management problem: A solution using evolutionary algorithms. IETE Technical Review 37(5) 540–548.

[51] Mohseni-Bonab SA, Rabiee A (2017) Modeling wind speed uncertainty in ORPD using Weibull distribution. Renewable Energy 101:131–140.

[52] Prisma Megantoro et al (2025) Modeling the uncertainties and active power generation of wind-solar energy with data acquisition from telemetry weather measurement. Results in Engineering 25:1–15.

[53] Liang X, Chai H, Ravishankar J (2022) Analytical methods of voltage stability in renewable dominated power systems: A review. Electricity 3(1) 75–107.

[54] Mokari M, Moradi MH (2020) Security constraint optimal reactive power dispatch under uncertainty in a wind integrated power system. 55th International Universities Power Engineering Conference (UPEC) pp.1–6.

[55] Zafar MH, Kowsalya M, Kothari DP (2025) Enhancing voltage stability through converter-supported DG. Energy Reports 13:397–423.

[56] Mohanty B, Tripathy S (2016) A teaching learning-based optimization technique for optimal location and size of DG in distribution network. J Electr Syst Inf Technol 3(1) 33–44.

[57] Hung Q, Mithulananthan N, Bansal RC (2013) Multiple distributed generators placement in primary distribution networks for loss reduction. IEEE Trans Ind Electron 60(4) 1700–1708.

[58] Ali S, Abd Elazim SM, Abdelaziz AY (2018) Optimal allocation and sizing of renewable distributed generation using ant lion optimization algorithm. Electr Eng 100:99–109.

[59] Quadri A, Bhowmick S, Joshi D (2018) A comprehensive technique for optimal allocation of distributed energy resources in radial distribution systems. Appl Energy 211:1245–1260.

[60] Ghanbari N (2018) Optimizing operation indices considering different types of distributed generation in microgrid applications. Energies 11(4) 1–19.

[61] Iqbal F et al (2018) Optimal placement of DG and DSTATCOM for loss reduction and voltage profile improvement. Alexandria Eng J 57(2) 755–765.

[62] Godha NR, Bapat VN, Korachagaon I (2020) Placement of distributed generation in distribution networks: A survey on different heuristic methods. Cham: Springer, 41–50.

[63] Moradi MH, Abedini M (2012) A combination of genetic algorithm and particle swarm optimization for optimal DG location and sizing in distribution systems. Electr Power Energy Syst 34(1) 66–74.

[64] Bagheri A, Habibzadeh A, Alizadeh SM (2011) Comparison of the effect of combination of different DG types on loss reduction using APSO algorithm. Can J Electr Electron Eng 2(10) 468–474.

[65] Jalili A, Taheri B (2020) Optimal sizing and sitting of distributed generations in power distribution networks using firefly algorithm. Technol Econ Smart Grids Sustain Energy 5(9) 1–14.

[66] Narain A, Srivastava SK (2015) An overview of facts devices used for reactive power compensation techniques. Power 4(12).

[67] Athamneh AA, Lee W-J (2006) Benefits of FACTS devices for power exchange among Jordanian interconnection with other countries. In 2006 IEEE Power Engineering Society General Meeting 7.

[68] Georgilakis PS, Hatziargyriou ND (2019) Unified power flow controllers in smart power systems: Models, methods, and future research. IET Smart Grid 2(1) 2–10.

[69] Iravani M, Maratukulam D (1994) Review of semiconductor-controlled (static) phase shifters for power systems applications. IEEE Trans Power Syst 9(4) 1833–1839.

[70] Das A, Dawn S, Gope S (2019) A review on optimal placement of FACTS devices. Int J Comput Intell & IoT 2(3).

[71] Kiran Kumar Ch, Sudheer Kumar M, Srirambabu V, Nagulmeera S (2014) A comparative analysis of UPFC as a power flow controller with applications. IOSR Journal of Electrical and Electronics Engineering 9:28–36.

[72] Gyugyi L, Sen Kalyan K, Schauder CD (1997) Static synchronous series compensator: A solid-state approach to the series compensation of transmission lines. IEEE Transactions on Power Delivery 12(1) 406–417.

[73] Kazemi A, Jamali S, Shateri H (2008) Measured impedance by distance relay for inter phase faults in presence of SSSC on a double circuit transmission line. TENCON-2008 IEEE Region 10 Conference.

[74] Cao G, Dong ZY, Wang Y, Zhang P (2007) VSC based series FACTS controllers for damping local mode oscillations. In 2007 IEEE Power Engineering Society General Meeting, Tampa, FL 1–7.

[75] Aswathi Krishna D, Sindhu MR (2016) Application of static synchronous compensator (STATCOM) to enhance voltage profile in IEEE Standard 5 Bus Transmission System. Indian Journal of Science and Technology 9:1–7.

[76] Beza M, Bongiorno M (2015) Comparison of two control approaches for stability enhancement using STATCOM with active power injection capability. In 2015 IEEE Energy Conversion Congress and Exposition (ECCE), Montreal, QC, Canada, pp.4721–4728.

[77] Hossain S, Rahman Khan A, Jannat-E-Noor (2014) Design of STATCOM for power system stability improvement. Global Journal of Research in Engineering: Electrical and Electronics Engineering 14:1–7.

[78] Kumar P (2015) Application of fact devices for voltage stability in a power system. In IEEE Sponsored 9th International Conference on Intelligent Systems and Control.

[79] Mishra S, Dash PK, Panda G (2000) TS-fuzzy controller for UPFC in a multimachine power system. IEE Proc-Gener Transm Distrib 147:15–22.

[80] Martins IM, Silva Fernando A, Pinto Sónia F, Martins Isménio E (2014) Sliding mode active and reactive power decoupled control for distributed power flow controllers. Electric Power Systems Research 112:65–73.

[81] Reddy MRS, Kumar MV (2013) Power quality improvement in DFIG based wind energy conversion system using UPFC. IOSR Journal of Engineering 3:46–54.

[82] Taher SA, Hemmati R, Abdolalipour A, Akbari S (2012) Comparison of different robust control methods in design of decentralized UPFC controllers. International Journal of Electrical Power & Energy Systems 43:173–184.

[83] Alajrash BH, Salem M, Swadi M, Senjyu T, Kamarol M, Motahhir S (2024) A comprehensive review of FACTS devices in modern power systems: Addressing power quality, optimal placement, and stability with renewable energy penetration. Energy Reports 11:5350–5371.

[84] Roshan S, Mirzaei M, Zareipour R (2020) Nonlinear programming-based placement of FACTS for voltage stability. IEEE Trans Power Syst 35(2) 891–900.

[85] Roselyn JP, Devaraj D, Dash SS (2014) Multi-objective genetic algorithm for voltage stability enhancement using rescheduling and FACTS devices. Ain Shams Engineering Journal 5(3) 789–801.

[86] Haldurai B, Kumar A (2016) Genetic algorithm-based optimization for FACTS deployment. Int J Eng Sci 4(3) 45–53.

[87] Gaur S, Mathew A (2018) FACTS device placement using PSO in IEEE test systems. Electric Power Components and Systems 46(11-12) 1264–1274.

[88] Shaheen HI, Rashed GI, Cheng SJ (2011) Optimal location and parameter setting of UPFC for enhancing power system security based on differential evolution algorithm. International Journal of Electrical Power & Energy Systems 33(1) 94–105.

[89] Sirjani R, Hosseini SH, Ranjbar AM (2012) Simulated annealing for optimal location of FACTS. IEEE Trans Power Delivery 27(2) 992–1000.

[90] Prakash S, Khatod DK (2016) Optimal sizing of FACTS using tabu search. Renewable and Sustainable Energy Reviews 25:300–309.
[91] Ahmad M, Sirjani R (2020) Hybrid analytical–metaheuristic strategies for FACTS placement. Energy Reports 10:1011–1020.
[92] Singh A, Mehta N, Sharma S (2010) Fuzzy logic based optimal placement of FACTS. International Journal of Electrical Power & Energy Systems 32(9) 998–1005.
[93] Bhayani P, Pandya V (2019) Hybrid optimization of multi-type FACTS placement. Energy Reports 7:1325–1333.
[94] Passino KM (2002) Bacterial foraging optimization. IEEE Control Systems Magazine 22(3) 52–67.
[95] El-Fergany AA, Hasanien HM (2015) Grey Wolf Optimizer for optimal allocation of FACTS devices. Engineering Science and Technology: An International Journal 18(3) 496–503.
[96] Hernandez J, Diaz M, Soto J (2013) FACTS optimal location using evolutionary programming. Electric Power Components and Systems 41(14) 1352–1364.
[97] Siddique M, Adeli H (2017) Grey wolf optimization and harmony search for power system design. Applied Soft Computing 64:369–390.
[98] Mirsaeidi S et al (2022) Modern metaheuristics for power system optimization. Sustainable Energy Technologies and Assessments 51:111–125.
[99] Zhou X, Zou L, Ma Y, Gao Z (2017) Research on impacts of the electric vehicles charging and discharging on power grid. 29th Chinese Control and Decision Conference (CCDC), pp.1398–1402.
[100] Lucas Alexandre, Bonavitacola Fausto, Kotsakis Evangelos, Fulli Gianluca (2015) Grid harmonic impact of multiple electric vehicle fast charging. Electric Power Syst Res 127:13–21.
[101] Delgado Joaquim, Faria Ricardo, Moura Pedro, de Almeida Aníbal T (2018) Impacts of plug-in electric vehicles in the Portuguese electrical grid. Transport Res Part D: Transport Environ 62:372–385.
[102] Williamson SS, Rathore AK, Musavi F (2015) Industrial electronics for electric transportation: current state of-the-art and future challenges‖. IEEE Trans Ind Electron 62:3021–3032.
[103] Grunditz EA, Thiringer T (2016) Performance analysis of current BEVs based on a comprehensive review of specifications. IEEE Trans Transp Electr 2:270–289.
[104] Freire R, Delgado J, Santos JM, de Almeida AT (2010) Integration of renewable energy generation with EV charging strategies to optimize grid load balancing, In 13th International IEEE Conference on Intelligent Transportation Systems 392–396.

[105] Von Jouanne A, Banerjee B (2001) Assessment of voltage unbalance. IEEE Trans Power Delivery 16(4) 782–790.

[106] Pillay P, Manyage M (2001) Definitions of voltage unbalance. IEEE Power Eng Rev 21(5) 49–51.

[107] Wu Xing, Aviquzzaman MD, Lin Zhenhong (2015) Analysis of plug-in hybrid electric vehicles' utility factors using GPS-based longitudinal travel data. Transport Res Part C: Emerging Technol 57:1–12.

[108] Shuaibu Hassan A, Sun Y, Wang Z (2020) Optimization techniques applied for optimal planning and integration of renewable energy sources based on distributed generation: recent trends. Cogent Engineering 7(1).

[109] Gunantara N (2018) A review of multi-objective optimization: methods and its applications. Cogent Engineering 5(1).

[110] Shwehdi MH, Mohamed SR, Devaraj D (2018) Optimal capacitor placement on West–East inter-tie in Saudi Arabia using genetic algorithm. Computers and Electrical Engineering 68:156–169.

[111] Liu Y, Yang J, Tang Y, Xu J, Sun Y, Chen Y, Peng X, Liao S (2019) Bilevel fuzzy stochastic expectation modelling and optimization for energy storage systems planning in virtual power plants. Journal of Renewable and Sustainable Energy 11(1) 014101.

[112] Storn R, Price K (1997) Differential evolution: A simple and efficient heuristic for global optimization over continuous spaces. Journal of Global Optimization 11(4) 341–359.

[113] Das S, Suganthan PN (2010) Differential evolution: a survey of the state-of-the-art. IEEE Transactions on Evolutionary Computation 15(1) 4–31.

[114] Huy PD, Ramachandaramurthy VK, Yong JY, Tan KM, Ekanayake JB (2020) Optimal placement, sizing and power factor of distributed generation: A comprehensive study spanning from the planning stage to the operation stage. Energy 195:117011.

[115] Lee S, Ayala HVH, Coelho LDS (2015) Capacitor placement of distribution systems using particle swarm optimization approaches. International Journal of Electrical Power and Energy Systems 64:839–851.

[116] Fard H, Jalilian A (2018) Optimal sizing and location of renewable energy-based DG units in distribution systems considering load growth. International Journal of Electrical Power and Energy Systems 101:356–370.

[117] Mosbah M, Mohammedi RD, Arif S, Hellal A (2017) Optimal of shunt capacitor placement and size in Algerian distribution network using particle swarm optimization. Proceedings of 2016 8th International Conference on Modelling, Identification and Control, ICMIC, University of MEDEA, Algeria, pp.192–197.

[118] Dong W, Li Y, Xiang J (2016) Optimal sizing of a stand-alone hybrid power system based on battery/hydrogen with an improved ant colony optimization. Energies 9(10) 785.

[119] Sanjay R, Jayabarathi T, Raghunathan T, Ramesh V, Mithulananthan N (2017) Optimal allocation of distributed generation using hybrid Grey Wolf Optimizer. IEEE Access 5:14807–14818.

[120] Ali A, Raisz D, Mahmoud K, Lehtonen M (2020) Optimal placement and sizing of uncertain PVS considering stochastic nature of PEVS. IEEE Transactions on Sustainable Energy 11(3) 1647–1656.

[121] Loganathan G, Geem ZW, Kim JH (2001) A new heuristic optimization algorithm: harmony search. Simulation 76(2) 60–68.

[122] Askarzadeh A (2017) Solving electrical power system problems by harmony search: A review. Artificial Intelligence Review 47(2) 217–251.

[123] Liu C, Abdulkareem SS, Rezvani A, Samad S, Aljojo N, Foong LK, Nishihara K (2020) Stochastic scheduling of a renewable-based microgrid in the presence of electric vehicles using modified harmony search algorithm with control policies. Sustainable Cities and Society 59:102183.

[124] Deb S, Tammi K, Gao X-Z, Kalita K, Mahanta P (2020) A hybrid multi-objective chicken swarm optimization and teaching learning-based algorithm for charging station placement problem. IEEE Access 8:92573–92590.

[125] Ehrgott M (2005) Multicriteria Optimization. Germany: Springer.

[126] Mirjalili S, Mirjalili SM, Lewis A (2014) Grey Wolf Optimizer. Advances in Engineering Software 69: 46–61.

[127] Roy SP et al (2022) Frequency control of GWO optimized two-area microgrid with TIDF-II, I-PD and I-TD. Sustainable Energy and Technological Advancements, pp.267–277.

[128] Tizhoosh HR (2005) Opposition-based learning: a new scheme for machine intelligence. International Conference on Computational Intelligence for Modelling, Control and Automation and International Conference on Intelligent Agents, Web Technologies and Internet Commerce, pp.695–701.

[129] Vita V (2017) Development of a decision-making algorithm for the optimum size and placement of distributed generation units in distribution networks. Energies 10(9) 1433.

[130] IRENA (2019) Innovation outlook: Smart charging for electric vehicles. International Renewable Energy Agency, Abu Dhabi, pp.1–138.

[131] Lee SH, Grainger JJ (1981) Optimum placement of fixed and switched capacitors on primary distribution feeders. IEEE Trans Power Appl Syst 100:345–352.

[132] Song YH, Wang GS, Johns AT, Wang PY (1997) Distribution network reconfiguration for loss reduction using fuzzy controlled evolutionary programming. Proc Gener Trans Distrib 144:345–350.

[133] Singh K, Yadav VK, Padhy NP, Sharma J (2013) Congestion management considering optimal placement of distributed generator in deregulated power system networks. Electr Power Compon Syst 42:13–22.

[134] Federico J, Gonzalez V, Lyra C (2005) Learning classifiers shape reactive power to decrease losses in power distribution networks. IEEE Power Eng Soc General Meet 1:557–562.

[135] Ackermann T, Andersson G, Söder L (2001) Distributed generation: A definition. Int J Electr Power Syst Res 57(3) 195–204.

[136] El-Zonkoly A (2011) Optimal placement of multi-distributed generation units including different load models using particle swarm optimization. IET Generation, Transmission and Distribution 12(3) 760–771.

[137] Ayres H, Freitas W, De Almeida M, da Silva L (2014) Method for determining the maximum allowable penetration level of distributed generation without steady-state voltage violations. IET Generation, Transmission and Distribution 14(5) 495–508.

[138] Chen P, Salcedo R, Zhu Q et al (2012) Analysis of voltage profile problems due to the penetration of distributed generation in low-voltage secondary distribution networks. IEEE Transactions on Power Delivery 8(1) 2020–2028.

[139] Singh R, Goswami S (2009) A genetic algorithm-based approach for optimal allocation of distributed generations in power systems for voltage sensitive loads. ARPN Journal of Engineering and Applied Sciences 25:78–87.

[140] Abu-Mouti F, El-Hawary M (2011) Optimal distributed generation allocation and sizing in distribution systems via artificial bee colony algorithm. IEEE Transactions on Power Delivery 17(11) 2090–2101.

[141] Aref A, Davoudi M, Seifi A, Ganjkhany I, Davoudi M (2012) Particle swarm optimization-based method for optimal placement and estimation of DG capacity in distribution networks. International Journal of Science & Technology 31:486–491.

[142] Ipinnimo O, Chowdhury S, Mitra J (2012) Intelligent voltage dip detection in power networks with distributed generation (DG). North American Power Symposium (NAPS), pp.1–6.

[143] Abdolabadi A, Najafi HR (2017) A new islanding scheme based on multi-objective optimization for distribution systems implemented with DGs. Electrical Engineering (ICEE) Iranian Conference, pp.1278–1283.

[144] Alarcon-Rodriguez A, Ault G, Galloway S (2010) Multi-objective planning of distributed energy resources: a review of the state-of-the-art. Renewable Sustainable Energy Rev 14:1353–1366.

[145] Erdinc O, Tascikaraoglu A, Paterakis NG, Dursun I, Sinim MC, Catala JPS (2017) Comprehensive optimization model for sizing and siting of DG units, EV charging stations and energy storage systems. IEEE Transactions on Smart Grid 12(2) 1–12.

[146] Biswas S, Goswami S, Chatterjee A (2012) Optimum distributed generation placement with voltage sag effect minimization. Energy Conversion and Management 12:163–174.

[147] Biswas S, Goswami S (2010) Genetic algorithm based optimal placement of distributed generation reducing loss and improving voltage sag performance. Proceedings of the International Conference on Advances in Electrical & Electronics, The Institute of Doctors Engineers and Scientists (IDES), pp.49–51.

[148] Pirouzi S, Zaghian M, Aghaei J et al (2022) Hybrid planning of distributed generation and distribution automation to improve reliability and operation indices. International Journal of Electrical Power & Energy Systems 135:107540.

[149] He Y, Wu H, Bi R et al (2022) Coordinated planning of distributed generation and soft open points in active distribution network based on complete information dynamic game. International Journal of Electrical Power & Energy Systems 138:107953.

[150] Abushamah H, Haghifam M, Bolandi T (2021) A novel approach for distributed generation expansion planning considering its added value compared with centralized generation expansion. Sustainable Energy, Grids and Networks 25:100417.

[151] Valencia A, Hincapie R, Gallego R (2021) Optimal location, selection, and operation of battery energy storage systems and renewable distributed generation in medium–low voltage distribution networks. Journal of Energy Storage 34:102158.

[152] Zangmo R, Sudabattula SK, Mishra S et al (2024) Optimal placement of renewable distributed generators and electric vehicles using multi-population evolution whale optimization algorithm. Scientific Reports 14(1) 28447.

[153] Dharavat N, Sudabattula SK, Suresh V (2022) Optimal integration of Distributed Generators (DGs) Shunt Capacitors (SCs) and Electric Vehicles (EVs) in a Distribution System (DS) using marine predator algorithm. International Journal of Renewable Energy Research (IJRER) 12:1805–1818.

[154] Dharavat N, Sudabattula SK, Velamuri S et al (2022) Optimal allocation of renewable distributed generators and electric vehicles in a distribution system using the political optimization algorithm. Energies 15(18) 6698.

[155] Mojarrad H, Gharehpetian GB, Rastegar H, Olamaeim J (2013) Optimal placement and sizing of DG (distributed generation) units in distribution networks by novel hybrid evolutionary algorithm. Energy 54(1) 129–138.

[156] Arya LD, Koshti A, Choube SC (2012) Distributed generation planning using differential evolution accounting voltage stability consideration. Inter Journal of Electrical Power & Energy Systems 42(1) 196–207.

[157] Bhatnagar R, Yadav A, Niazi KR (2019) Multi-objective optimal allocation and sizing of distributed generation using an improved differential evolution algorithm. Intern Journal of Electrical Power & Energy Systems 105:594–606.

[158] Rafee SM, Reddy AS (2021) Enhancing System Loadability with Multiple FACTS Devices Using Artificial Bee Colony Algorithm. Springer, Singapore. 700:311–322.

[159] Kaur GD, Singh H (2021) Power transmission fault analysis using the concept of firefly optimization algorithm along with FACTS devices. International Journal of Advanced Computer Management Studies 11:24–32.

[160] Amarendra A, Srinivas LR, Srinivasa Rao R (2022) Power system security enhancement in FACTS devices based on yin–yang pair optimization algorithm. Soft Computing 26:6265–6291.

[161] Khan NH et al (2021) A novel modified lightning attachment procedure optimization technique for optimal allocation of the FACTS devices in power systems. IEEE Access 9:47976–47997.

[162] Amarendra A, Srinivas LR, Rao RS (2021) Security enhancement in power system using FACTS devices and atom search optimization algorithm. EAI Endorsed Transactions on Energy Web 8(36) e9.

[163] Kumar TT, Satyanara RVS (2018) Enhancing power system security: A multi-objective optimal approach to identify the location and size of SVC. IUP Journal of Electrical and Electronics Engineering 11:45–48.

[164] Kumar BS, Suryakalavathi M, Kumar GVN (2018) Thyristor controlled series compensator based optimal reallocation of generators for contingency management. ECTI Transactions on Electrical Engineering Electronics and Communications 16:30–38.

[165] Chamba A, Barrera-Singaña C, Arcos H (2023) Optimal reactive power dispatch in electric transmission systems using the multiagent model with volt-VAR control. Energies 16:1–25.

[166] Karmakar N, Bhattacharyya B (2023) Optimal reactive power planning under active and reactive power steady state load model. e-Prime Adv Electr Eng Electron Energy 5:1–16.

[167] Shaheen MAM, Hasanien HM, Alkuhayli A (2021) A novel hybrid GWO-PSO optimization technique for optimal reactive power dispatch problem solution. Ain Shams Eng J 12:621–630.

[168] Premkumar M, Tengku Hashim TJ, Ravichandran S, Sin TC, Chandran R, Alsoud AR, Jangir P (2024) Optimal operation and control of hybrid power systems with stochastic renewables and FACTS devices: An intelligent multi-objective optimization approach. Alexandria Engineering Journal 93:90–113.

[169] Sulaiman MH, Mustaffa Z (2024) Hyper-heuristic strategies for optimal power flow problem with FACTS devices allocation in wind power integrated system. Results in Control and Optimization 14:100373.

[170] Jangir P, Ezugwu AE et al (2024) Precision parameter estimation in proton exchange membrane fuel cells using depth information enhanced differential evolution. Sci Reports 14:29591.

[171] Gyugyi L (1992) Unified power-flow control concept for flexible ac transmission systems. IEE Proceedings C Generation Transmission and Distribution 139:323–331.

[172] Pal K, Verma K, Gandotra R (2024) Optimal location of FACTS devices with EVCS in power system network using PSO. e-Prime 7:1-11. https://doi.org/10.1016/j.prime.2024.100482

Index

For Product Safety Concerns and Information please contact our
EU representative GPSR@taylorandfrancis.com Taylor & Francis
Verlag GmbH, Kaufingerstraße 24, 80331 München, Germany